# Gibson

ANDRÉ DUCHOSSOIR

EXCLUSIVELY DISTRIBUTED BY
HAL•LEONARD™ CORPORATION
7777 W. BLUEMOUND RD. P.O. BOX 13819 MILWAUKEE, WI 53213

# PREFACE

Different articles published these last years in "Disc" magazine have shown that readers are interested in what some respectfully call "old" guitars. We felt that this interest had only been imperfectly catered for by the various publications in circulation, and that it would be timely to approach, in a more complete way, certain subjects in book form.

As regards guitars, one name immediately came to our mind because of its influence and the magic it creates: that name is Gibson. Naturally, the idea that there is only Gibson is very far from us, but whether we want to admit it or not, the Number One manufacturer, all categories combined, is whithout a doubt Gibson...

No other manufacturer can pride itself on having the prestige, the past or the creativity of Gibson. If there must be history, then a work on Gibson is indispensable.

We have accordingly decided to restrict the subject to only electric guitars, as we considered it difficult to treat the entire history of Gibson without resorting to a work of several hundred pages which, in another respect, would have entailed several years of research and preparation.

In fact, only some American articles by competent people, such as George Gruhn or Tom Wheeler, have sketched what we hope to do in more details in this present work. It is furthermore paradoxical to realize that no American expert has ever thought of publishing this type of study, as there is certainly no lack of potential authors.

Only Julius Bellson, the semi-official historian of Gibson, published "The Gibson Story" (several years ago) in which the origins and the progression of Gibson are faithfully reported, with, however, greater attention given to the characters of the different periods than to the models of the brand.

Naturally, "The Gibson Story" is recommended to all Gibson enthusiasts, who will especially appreciate the documents relating to the pre-War period.

Our purpose is therefore to present, as accurately as possible, the different Gibson electric models hence our title "Gibson Electrics". However, only guitars (in the strict sense) and electric basses will be studied in depth and, except for anecdotal mention, mandolins, banjos and other Hawaiian guitars, will be left aside. By the same token, "Epiphone" or "Kalamazoo" instruments will not be examined in details in this book.

Furthermore, we have decided to divide the narrative into two distinct volumes, which will respectively deal with the electric models from the beginnings until to 1961 (volume 1), and from 1961 up to 1981 (volume 2). The chronological thread seems the most natural under the circumstances, and besides, it allows one to appreciate much better the progression of Gibson through the years, something a "strict" typology by instrument would have badly rendered.

It goes without saying that this project has necessitated a lot of research and, while gathering the basic documentation, we have constantly looked to verify our information and cross-check it.

Naturally, this work would not have been possible without the active collaboration of numerous people, particularly in the United States.

We would, therefore, like to give our warmest thanks to Norlin and Gibson for their close cooperation, which was expressed in particular during two profitable stays at their factory in Kalamazoo, and a visit of the relatively new plant in Nashville. Robert McRann, David Sutton and Arthur Boguse of Norlin were more than willing to help us in our proceedings, and we are grateful to them for having believed in this project.

The very friendly welcome of Jim Deurloo, plant manager in Kalamazoo and of his team, undeniably facilitated our research to complete the information we had already gathered.

It is useless to emphasize how much we appreciated the possibility we were given to consult certain factory registers, in order to extract valuable information. Along with Jim Deurloo, we want particularly to thank Ken Killman, Abe Wechter, Tim Shaw and many others whom we know only by their first names. And finally a very special mention for our guide Gerald Bergeon, the oldest active employee of Gibson who began his career in Kalamazoo in 1933 !

Gerald greatly contributed to the efficiency of our stay by arranging, in particular, for us to get long interviews with Ted MacCarty, who was president of Gibson from 1950 to 1966, and with Walter Fuller who was from 1933 to 1975 the main "wizard" behind Gibson electronics. Both were kind enough to spend a few hours in our company, to answer questions we were eager to ask them, and we want to thank them wholeheartedly for their contribution.

In another respect, we must admit that it would have been inconceivable to write anything about Gibson, without consulting Julius Bellson, who was good enough to receive us at his home and allow us to consult his numerous records. Mr Bellson started at Gibson in 1935 and he is often considered as the "official" historian of the company. Is it necessary to add that as such he possesses very impressive documents !

Besides these people, we would equally like to express our warmest thanks to George Gruhn, the famous expert from Nashville, who lavished both encouragement and information in order to make this work a reality. We must also point out that a great number of photos that appear in the two volumes were taken at his store on Broadway, during our different stays in Nashville. In addition, George was equally willing to let us consult his records and personal documents ; a wealth of nearly twenty years of experience in vintage guitars.

We are grateful to Tony Dukes for the various documents he was willing to lend us so as to illustrate this book. Tony "Dukes Deluxe", who lives in Texas is specialized in the research of rare instruments, and he counts among his famous clients groups such as ZZ Top and the Eagles.

Herschel Blankenship of Schecter Research, Inc. did help us tremendously in providing superb documents on some Gibson "rare birds" and through him we would like to extend our thanks to Robb Lawrence, Frank Lucido (of California Guitar), Douglas Chandler and Alan Rogan.

Finally, to close this chapter of acknowledgements from the American side of the Atlantic, we would like to mention certain retailers of 48th Street, in New-York, such as the members of the Friedman family, who kindly allowed us to photograph a few models in their shops.

Besides this collaboration from America, this project equally benefitted in France from the active help of people who it would be unfair not to cite. In the first rank, we are pleased to thank the Jacobacci brothers, who have no peers for "making an old guitar speak", and whose everyday collaboration and knowledge permitted us to advance towards our goal.

Several collectors were also kind enough to let us photograph their guitars, in order to contribute to a better illustration of this work. Among them, we are most grateful towards our friend Daniel Marc Ducros, as well as "Slim" Pezin of Voyage.

Lastly, we would especially like to thank Rene Duchossoir, without whom the author might never have known what a Gibson guitar was !

And now the only thing left is to hope that guitar enthusiasts in general and Gibson "fans" in particular will be satisfied with these pages, relating the story of the Gibson Electrics.

André Duchossoir
March 1981

# GIBSON ELECTRICS

## from the origins up to 1961

## CONTENTS

# FOREWORD

# ONCE UPON A TIME... FROM ORVILLE GIBSON... TO NORLIN

If the name Gibson has been well-known and respected for a long time throughout the world, its history, on the other hand, is generally little known.

It seems therefore inconceivable to us not to sketch as a sort of preamble the most striking facts of this history, beginning naturally with Orville H. Gibson.

## ORVILLE H. GIBSON

Orville H. Gibson was born in 1856 in Chateaugay in the state of New-York. His family was of English origin and, after immigrating, his father, John Gibson settled in the United States near New-York. The reasons why John Gibson left England are not precisely known and he himself always refused to discuss the matter. Be that as it may, the young man Orville Gibson found himself later on in the state of Michigan, in Kalamazoo to be exact, as a clerk in a shoe store. At this time his favorite pastime was already, wood-working, and very quickly, he assigned himself the task of improving the quality of mandolins, which were very fashionable instruments at the time. He especially wanted to create a mandolin applying the principles defined by Stradivarius in the manufacturing of violins with a carved top and back. These first models were thus conceived at the end of the 1880's, entirely by hand, with only the help of the tools he was accustomed to using for woodworking. As for the supply of raw materials, Orville Gibson showed a clear preference for any old furniture he could find whose quality and low degree of humidity he appreciated.

The different pieces created by Orville Gibson did not take long to find buyers, considering their quality and originality. In fact, each model was different from the preceding one as Orville naturally was trying to advance in the application to mandolins, and then to guitars of the principles, governing up to that time, the making of violins. A little later, around 1894, he abandoned for good his job as salesclerk to set himself up in business in a guitar-making workshop. He then began to work in a continuous way on two or three instruments at the same time, either guitar or mandolin. His production was, to be sure, somewhat larger but it remained on a perfectly small scale. Moreover, as before, it was quite rare that two models were exactly identical, and this was even more so as he worked more often than not on special order. Orville Gibson's instruments, besides their innovative conception for that time, were characterized by their very refined finishing touches, in particular with superb pearl inlays (see for example the famous butterfly inlaid guitar created for Mrs. D.O. Boudeman). The various pearl inlays then used by Orville Gibson were made by a Turkish manufacturer based in Michigan and this accounts for the star and crescent symbol featured on most of the instruments he made at the time. It must be noted that Orville Gibson's guitars were of an unusual size for their time, being much wider than a Martin or à Washburn for example. Besides this, most of his instruments were equipped with a sort of tube-like hollow neck so as to favor the resonance.

In 1899, Orville Gibson's workshop was at 104 East Main Street in Kalamazoo and his reputation grew to such a point that a group of local business-men offered him to set up a company which, while increasing his production capacity, would allow him to enlarge his clientele and improve the spread of instruments created according to his principles.

So Orville Gibson accepted the offer made to him by Sylvo Reams, Lewis A. Williams, Leroy Hornbeck, Samuel H. Van Horn and John W. Adams, and in 1902, the Gibson Mandolin Guitar Manufacturing Company Ltd. was founded. John Adams was chairman — and was to remain so until 1944 — while Sylvo Reams was secretary and production manager and Lewis Williams responsible, among other things, for advertising and in particular for the numerous slogans used at the beginning of the century to promote the brand. Lewis Williams was also going to play a large part in the development of certain ideas relating to acoustics.

As for Orville Gibson, according to the terms of his contract, he had to impart his knowledge of stringed instruments for at least two years to the thirteen employees of the new company. In addition, he naturally was supposed to continue designing new models. In 1906, the compagny's capital was increased from $ 12,000.00 to $ 40,000.00 and it became known as the Gibson Mandolin Guitar Company when it moved to 116 East Exchange Place in Kalamazoo. The beginning of the twentieth century was going to reveal itself as very favorable for the mandolin and orchestras centered around this instrument were numerous at that time. Of course, the Gibson "A" and "F" models as well as the Mandolas and Mando-Cellos found an excellent market there which strongly contributed to the development of the brand.

In 1911, the Gibson Company moved to 523 East Harrisson Court, and in fact, a little later, it proceeded to purchase land on Parsons Street, where the construction of a new factory began in 1916.

In the meantime, on April 12, 1915, the Gibson Mandolin Guitar Company had concluded a new agreement with Orville Gibson allowing it to manufacture stringed instruments and other products under the Gibson name, in exchange for the payment of a life-time royalty. In fact, this decision can be explained by the declining health of Orville Gibson who, was to die shortly after of chronic endocarditis on August 19, 1918 in Ogdenburg... The creator who gave birth to the Gibson legend disappeared but the name was already promised to a greater glory.

## GIBSON INC.

In July 1917, the new premises located on 225 Parsons Street in Kalamazoo were inaugurated and since then Gibson guitars have always been manufactured at the same address... undoubtedly a part of the Gibson heritage.

At the end of World War I, which did not especially affect the production of the company, mandolins saw their popularity decline slightly in favour of the banjo, and-to a lesser degree-the orchestra type guitar.

The first Gibson banjos were thus introduced in 1918 to respond to this new demand of a public fond of marching songs.

The following year, Gibson was to grow rich from a remarkable contribution in the person of Lloyd A. Loar who came to work at the factory by the end of 1919.

Born in 1886, Lloyd Loar was a brilliant and multitalented personality, as he was at the same time a musician, author, composer, engineer, teacher and even more : very quickly, he was assigned full responsibility for most experimental work, design, customer service, application for patents, promotion and demonstration, plus other duties as required.

Without a doubt more was attibuted to Lloyd Loar than he really did to the detriment of people such as George D. Laurian or Lewis A. Williams, but he however remains the great craftsman behind the "Master Model" series which includes the F-5 Mandolin, the L-5 guitar, and K-5 Mando-Cello, the H-5 mandola or the Mastertone banjo. He also originated numerous accessories and improvements on stringed instruments during his stay at the Gibson factory. Lloyd Loar was even ready to go much further, as we will see later on in more details, especially as regards the amplification of musical stringed instruments.

The L-5 guitar was to undergo several modifications after its introduction in 1923, but it still remains today one of the greatest achievements in the field of acoustic guitars, and a standard of comparison for musicians.

Orville H. Gibson
(1856-1918)

KALAMAZOO,

Lloyd A. Loar

Lloyd A. Loar
Master of Music

The Kalamazoo plant
in the early twenties

THE DAYLIGHT PLANT OF
The Gibson Mandolin-Guitar Company
World's Largest Manufacturers
of Exclusively High Grade
Fretted Instruments

1915 style "0" Artist's model with its fleur-de-lys inlaid in the Headstock.

A young Orville Gibson posing with a guitar.
As suggested by the position of the strings on the instrument, Orville Gibson was in all probability left handed.

Unfortunately, Loar was — according to the well-known formula — "too far ahead of his time" and it seems that a disagreement with Guy Hart, who became the company secretary and general manager in 1924, lead him to leave the company "prematurely" at the end of December of that same year. The short passage of Lloyd Loar did, none the less, strongly mark Gibson's progession.

Shortly after the arrival of Loar, Thaddeus McHugh perfected, and then patented around 1922, the adjustable metal reinforced truss rod for the neck, which was fundamental to the development of the modern guitar. This invention permitted the necks of the Gibson instruments to be considerably slimmed and streamlined for easier playing in the 1920's. Since that time, the patent has fallen into the public domain and all "modern" guitars — Gibson or others — are today equipped with truss rods the idea of which goes back more than fifty years.

It is also at the beginning of the 1920's that Gibson began to produce its own strings for mandolins, guitars or banjos, marketed naturally under the brand name.

The early part of the 1920's marked the end of the mandolin era and the beginning of the banjo era, in which Gibson shined on just as brightly thanks to the models of the "Mastertone" series such as the "All American", "Florentine" and other "Bella Voce" or "Granada". At this time, the name of the company was shortened from the Gibson Mandolin Guitar Company to Gibson Inc. for obvious reasons.

Then, in 1926, Gibson presented its first "Flat Top" guitars and in particular the famous Nick Lucas model. "The" disappeared in front of "Gibson" on the headstock at the beginning of the 1930's, practically at the time when the guitar began to take permanently the place of the banjo to become the "popular" instrument above all others.

After having conceived the first "Jumbo" guitars around 1934, Gibson introduced in 1935 a complete and revamped line of guitars with carved tops and "F" sound holes instead of a round sound hole, after the fashion of Loar's famous L-5. The L-5 was equally reviewed and its body widened to 17" instead of 16", Gibson presenting simultaneously other models of a similar format, the L-12, L-10, and L-7. However, the great novelty of the time was the "Super 400" of a size called "Super Grand Auditorium" with its body of more than 18" wide. The designation of this model was simply taken from its rather astronomical price for the time... $ 400.00 !

But already, another still more important revolution was being prepared with the introduction of the electric Hawaiian guitar at the beginning of 1935, followed shortly after by the electric acoustic guitar (Electric Spanish). Gibson in its turn had just launched the electric guitar. The beginnings were surely going to be timid, but the process leading to the creation of a new family of instruments was set into motion in an irreversible way.

The first violins in 1937, then the first classical guitars in 1939 contributed to definitely establish Gibson as the largest manufacturer of professional quality stringed instruments in the world at that time.

World War II was obviously to stop somewhat the impetus taken by Gibson, as, starting in 1942, all musical instrument production, was more or less curtailed until the end of 1945. Only some models were still assembled during this period with the aid of parts and elements already in stock.

Because of its qualified workmanship Gibson was assigned several sub-contracts both in the mechanical or electrical field in order to support America's war effort.

# C.M.I.

In 1944, Chicago Musical Instruments, located at 3 East Adams Street in Chicago, acquired a controlling interest in Gibson Inc., and Maurice H. Berlin, president of C.M.I., became general secretary and treasurer of Gibson, while Guy Hart continued as general manager. From this date on, the Gibson sales department was permanently located in Chicago while the Kalamazoo factory concentrated its efforts on designing and manufacturing musical instruments.

The period immediately following the War would mark the irresistible rise of the electric guitar, but this is a subject we will come back to in more details throughout this work. After a period of restrictions due to the War, the demand for instruments was almost phe-

"EVERY ONE A 'GIBSON'-ITE"
THE MUSICAL NOSSES

The Gibson Mandolin-Guitar Co.,
Kalamazoo, Mich.

New York.

Gentlemen: I wish to add a few words of praise to your already long list of testimonials. As you know, we always pay full cash price for all of our instruments, and are under no obligations to any firm, but you have given us such an excellent article that I feel it a duty I owe to you to express our appreciation and approval of the "Gibson" instruments.

Our work being mostly with big musical productions, we require the very best instruments obtainable, and I do not see how our present set of "Gibsons" could be improved upon. We have been using them for about two years now and have had ample time to test them under all kinds of conditions. The last production with which we were identified, we had to play them with a chorus of thirty, and an orchestra of eighteen, yet we could be heard above all that volume, which would have been impossible with the old-style Mandolin.

Thanking you for making our success possible, and wishing you every success, I am,

Yours truly,
PERD NOSS,
The Musical Nosses.

The Musical Nosses, one of the numerous mandolin orchestras of the early twenties.

The original SUPER 400 introduced in the mid-thirties (with non original pick guard).

L-5 Master model

nomenal, with, in particular, the popularity of "Hawaiian" guitars. Thanks to the additional buildings erected in 1945, Gibson was in a position to meet this unprecedented demand, at a time when the need for music was expanding by leaps and bounds.

In March 1948, Theodore M. Mac Carty joined the Gibson staff, where he would be elected president and general manager after the retirement of Guy Hart in 1950.

Ted MacCarty worked in the tracks laid down by his predecessors, but it can be stated, beyond the shadow of a doubt, that he contributed even more than any other to establish internationally the name of Gibson to its advantage, if only for the numerous original models that saw the light of day during his presidency.

Thus, in 1952, after having overcome diverse reservations in opposition to this new concept of "Solid Body" guitars, Gibson, thanks to Ted MacCarty, introduced the first model of the famous Les Paul series.

It is perfectly superfluous to insist on the unequaled success of this series, which, over the years, would even be identified with the image of the electric guitar.

Then, in 1958, so as in a way to fill the gap existing between the electric spanish guitars and the "solid body" ones, Gibson presented, once again under Ted MacCarty's instigation, its semi-solid series whose principle, it is enough to say, has since been copied by all of Gibson's competitors.

The 1950's, thus, witnessed the creation of new models, destined to follow the evolution of the different musical currents, and meet the needs of a new generation of players. In 1958, an ever increasing demand justified the spectacular enlargement of the factory. In 1935 and 1945, Gibson had already erected different additional buildings to the original plant on Parsons Street, but the new premises built in 1950, and especially the one built in 1960 were to more than double the capacity of Gibson, and demonstrate the conquering vitality of the company.

In 1962, a second plant located on East Ranson Street was inaugurated to shelter Gibson's electronic activities, such as amplifiers and pick-ups. Walter Fuller was appointed manager of this new plant while Richard Evans became chief electronic engineer.

Afterwards, in 1964, a third unit was even created in Kalamazoo to receive the electronics division while the number-2 factory was used in conjunction with the main factory on Parsons Street for the manufacturing of the instruments, including Epiphone models.

As a matter of fact, following financial problems in the mid-fifties, Orfie Stathopoulo had decided to sell the Epiphone company founded in the early 1920's by his father, and named after his brother Epi. Epiphone up until then, produced a range of quality instruments, in direct competition with the Gibson models.

In 1957, Gibson purchased the rights to the trade name, as well as the patents and the design copyrights necessary for the making of the models.

The first Epiphones manufactured by Gibson were brought out in 1958 and offered through a network of franchised dealers competitive with the normal Gibson network. After the enlargement of the factory premises, the different Epiphone models were produced in Kalamazoo simultaneously with the Gibson range. This parallel manufacturing was stopped in 1969 when Gibson decided to consecrate its full potential to only Gibson models, and the name Epiphone was applied, starting in 1970, to instruments made in Japan.

The sales of guitars registered a fantastic progression at the beginning of the 1960's, which saw the success of semi-solid guitars and especially the take-off of the "solid body" guitars thanks to the SG series or Melody Maker types whose sales amounted to thousands of units each year. The culminating point of what is generally called the first "guitar boom" is situated around 1965, and under the circumstances Gibson's sales doubled from January 1964 to June 1966 ! that is to say a record progression of 1,250 % since 1949 !

In November 1965, Ted MacCarty and John Huis gave their resignations in order to devote themselves, after so much effort for Gibson, to the management of a small accessories business that they had just bought from Paul Bigsby. In fact, they were to stay at their post until June 30, 1966, when Al Stanley and Ed Strand briefly succeeded them. Then in February 1968, Stanley Rendell, vice-president of CMI since 1963, became in turn pre-

The old building on Parsons street as it appears today more than 60 years after it was first inaugurated.

A second plant has been erected in Nashville, in the early part of the seventies.

An aerial view of the premises in Kalamazoo with the dates of erection of the different buildings in order to show the growth pattern.

sident of Gibson with, starting in 1971, Tom Fetters as assistant.

In another respect, it is fitting to point out that in September 1967, a young guitarist named Bruce J. Bolen had equally joined the ranks of Gibson to become the "house demonstrator" after brilliantly passing the entrance examination set up by Maurice Berlin.

# NORLIN

At the end of 1969, more exactly on December 22, an official statement announced to the C.M.I. employees — and consequently to those at Gibson — that E.C.L. Industries Inc. (founded in 1913) had just taken control of C.M.I. with more than 90 % of the capital.

For the public, Gibson Inc. remained under the control of C.M.I. until around 1974, when the name Norlin appeared.

Norlin is the contraction of H. **NOR**ton Stevens, president of E.C.L. Industries, and Maurice M. Ber**LIN**, president of C.M.I.. Gibson thus became a subsidiary of Norlin Musical Instruments, itself a member of Norlin Industries, whose activities are numerous as, besides musical instruments (Gibson, Moog, Lowrey...), Norlin deals in quartz crystals, tungsten equipment and even... beer ! The group, as such, realized a turnover in 1978 of nearly 270 m$ U.S.

The arrival of E.C.L. Industries, and then of Norlin, gave a new impetus to Gibson, which was to be shown in the introduction of a new breed of models starting in 1972, such as the L-5S, L-6S, and L-9S, then later on in radically original creations, like the "RD" series.

In 1974, a new factory was erected in Nashville, one of the capitals of American music, to allow Gibson to better absorb the growth of its activity. After initially being destined for, among other things, the making of the new "Mark" acoustic guitars, the Nashville plant henceforth concentrates on the production of "solid body" guitars, while Kalamazoo can actually make all the models and operate a little like a regulator according to the market's evolution.

In the meantime Stan Rendell left in 1976, and Carl Spinosa was appointed to the head of Kalamazoo, with Chuck Schneider directly responsible on the Norlin side. As for Whitey Morrison, he had taken charge of the new Nashville unit.

Then in 1978, James Deurloo — with Gibson for nearly 20 years — took over the helm from Carl Spinosa, while Robert McRann replaced Chuck Schneider. Also in 1978 Bruce Bolen officially became head of the "Research and Development" department, when for numerous years, he had already been the originator of most of the new models...

Finally, at the end of 1979, we learned that Martin Locke, formerly with Lowrey, replaced Robert McRann to become the new president of Gibson, which henceforth makes up a direct and independent division of Norlin Industries.

On the threshold of the 1980's, the Gibson name still possesses the same power and magic for all guitarists, amateur or professional. And each Gibson employee is perfectly aware of its heritage, as well as of the difficulty involved in surpassing himself in order to maintain the reputation it has. Be that as it may, there are many who will bet that in the years to come progress in the field of guitars will still come from Kalamazoo or Nashville.

To all those interested in a much more detailed history of Gibson, the reading of Julius Bellson's book, "The Gibson Story", is highly recommended, if only to better render justice to all those who helped to make the Gibson name what it is today.

For the moment, we will examine in more details the different phases in the evolution of the electric guitar at Gisbson and the numerous models issued throughout the years.

# CHAPTER 1

# THE PRE-WAR PERIOD
# THE BEGINNINGS
# OF THE ELECTRIC GUITAR

After having "followed" the mandolin, then the banjo as the "instrument of the people", the guitar quickly found itself confronted with a major problem... being heard! This problem originates from the structure of the acoustic guitar, and what could be termed as its natural power, relatively weak, compared to that of other instruments commonly found in an orchestra. Of course, in the absence of an orchestra, this problem is not excessively distrubing, but the evolution of musical tastes since the beginning of the twentieth century — and particularly since the late 1920's — was to make it more and more indispensible in certain contexts, to amplify the acoustic guitar.

## THE ORIGINS OF THE ELECTRIC GUITAR

Without entering into profound musical considerations, let us say in brief, that dance music, as well as jazz, are at the origin of the need to amplify the guitar, since both generally imply the presence of an orchestra.

Thus, dance music brought about the creation of the famous "big bands" in which the unamplified voice of the guitar, in another respect confined solely to a rhythmic role, had a lot of difficulty making itself heard. This explains in a large part the constant enlarging of the dimensions of acoustic guitars at this time, so as to increase their power. The "L-5", conceived in 1923 by Lloyd Loar, saw its width carried from 16 1/4" to 17" in 1935, while in the same year, Gibson introduced the famous "Super 400" with its "Super Grand Auditorium" 18 1/2" wide body. Elmer Stromberg, to mention only him, even offered a model designated Master 400 with a 19" wide body!

It is equally important to point out that aside from its composition, the very places where an orchestra was to perform, night clubs, or dance halls were often noisy and hardly contributed to the improvement of a natural imbalance in power. It is actually easier to hear a trumpet solo than an acoustic guitar amidst the distribution of drinks, or the noise of conversations.

The problems were exactly the same for a jazz guitarist, in the respect that his instrument in no way allowed him to have a place among the soloists, and relegated him, as a consequence, to the simple rank of accompanist. Moreover this "physical" restriction was doubly increased as a sort of "mental" one, as no guitarist then was in a position to take a chorus like the traditionally solo instruments.

In 1928, the black guitarist Lonnie Johnson, however, succeeded in a recording with the Duke Ellington orchestra, in which he took an acoustic lead entitled "The Mooche". He was furthermore, much before this recording, to inspire Eddie Lang, who was, in the early 1930's, the most famous jazz guitarist of the time, and above all the first to really take the guitar out of its "ghetto".

These diverse reasons therefore lead a certain number of guitarists to "amplify" the sound of their instruments, to allow them to be better heard and to be at least on an equal footing "with the others". Naturally, from the "amplified" guitar to the "electric" guitar, there was only one step quickly taken by people like Eddie Durham and Les Paul, or the guitarists of some of the "Country Western" orchestras like "Milton Brown and his musical Brownies" or "Bob Wills and his Texas Playboys".

It is difficult to ascertain who was the first, known or unknown guitarist, to play an electric guitar. Eddie Durham is, however, recognized as the first guitarist to have recorded a solo on an electric guitar, in 1938, with the group "Kansas City Six". It is, furthermore, this same Eddie Durham who in 1937 met, in Oklahoma City during a tour with Count Basie, a young man named Charlie Christian and introduced him to the electric guitar, and the manner in which it could be put to use!

With Charlie Christian, the "modern" guitar was to find its voice, and lay down its first milestones both as regards the form or the substance of a new style of guitar playing.

## THE FIRST GIBSON ATTEMPTS

And yet, much before Charlie Christian or Eddie Durham, a man had already guessed the potential of the electric instrument, or more exactly the virtues of amplification by adding a pick-up... this man was Lloyd A. Loar...

As a matter of fact, during his short stay at Gibson from late 1919 to 1924, Loar had already initiated some trials in the electrification of instruments. And if, as we have seen, it is difficult to know who was the first electric guitarist, there is practically no doubt that Lloyd Loar was the first to imagine a pick-up being able to adapt itself to a stringed instrument.

None of the experimental pick-ups created by this great pioneer have been kept for sure, but it is clear that they were of an electrostatic type and not electromagnetic. In addition, these pick-ups were characterized by their very high impedance, which, with the rudimentary process used to create the current meant to be amplified, necessitated a very short cable between the instrument and the amplifier. Lastly, they were also considered very sensitive to the surrounding humidity.

Lloyd Loar tried to convince the Gibson's management to introduce "electrified" stringed instruments. Unfortunately for him, Loar was really "years ahead of his time" and a quick investigation showed that neither the public, nor the retailers and, consequently the Gibson sales force, were ready to accept this revolutionary discovery.

To put it bluntly, the electric guitar "market" did not exist in 1924 and Gibson logically decided not to persue the idea or any research in this field. The differences in the opinions of Lloyd Loar and Guy Hart, who became secretary and general manager in 1924, were perhaps at the origin of the former's contract not being renewed at the end of that year. Loar preferred to leave the company with L.A. Williams in order to continue his research more freely. Later on, after having occupied different posts as a consultant or as a teacher, he was to found the "Acousti-Lectric" company in 1934, which became the "Vivi-Tone" company in 1936. The different "Vivi-Tone" models preserved to this day are striking proof of Lloyd Loar's original and precursory spirit.

During the 1920's no Gibson catalog presented any electric musical instrument, nevertheless, today it is practically accepted that some electric models carrying the Gibson name were conceived at the time, if only as prototypes. Julius Bellson, the author of "The Gibson Story" and the semi-official historian of the company kindly gave us a photograph of what he thinks to be the very first electric guitar created by Gibson, in view of a possible commercialization. Gibson would have sent then a brochure with a reproduction of this instrument to a certain number of dealers and agents asking for their comments. According to Mr. Bellson, this brochure reached him during the 1920's, while he was still living in Minneapolis, and thus much before he joined Gibson in 1935. The exact date of this document can therefore be estimated between 1924 and 1935, but it is difficult to be more precise as, obviously, the pick-up is of an electrostatic type, glued under the top near the bridge thanks to a thin sheet of cork.

This instrument is believed to be the very first electric guitar officially perfected by Gibson in the twenties. We are indebted to Julius Bellson for this rare photograph extracted from his personal archives.

It is, therefore, a pick-up identical to those originated by Lloyd Loar, but is it really a model created by Loar ? It is extremely difficult to confirm such an assumption because the guitar corresponds to a "L-4" in its late 1920's-early 1930's version, or an early "L-50" with a round sound hole. The neck joins the body at the fourteenth fret and above all the name inlaid on the peg-head shows "Gibson" and not "The Gibson".

It seems reasonable to think that the model illustrated was probably conceived around the very early 1930's, for lack of additional precisions. At any rate, Walter Fuller, who in 1933 was assigned the task of proceeding with the "amplification" of a guitar, and who was until 1975, closely associated with the different pick-ups produced by Gibson, told us he did not know of the existence of this peculiar instrument. Consequently, it could well be a survivor, of the Loar period, and of his first attempts to electrify a stringed instrument.

Of course, this electric "L-4" (?) remained without any follow-up, and it is solely at the beginning of the 1930's that Gibson became interested in the problem of amplification...

Be that as it may, Gibson was unquestionably the first company to have conceived an electric guitar !

# THE FIRST COMMERCIALIZED ELECTRIC GUITAR

The evolution of musical trends, as well as the first steps of certain manufacturers towards an "electric" guitar, prompted Gibson to resume the project, and to perfect in a relatively short lapse of time complete line of electric guitars.

As a matter of fact, Rickenbacker commercialized in 1931 its famous "frying pan" designed by George Beauchamp and Paul Barth. It was an electric Hawaiian guitar with 7 strings (model A-22 and A-25), characterized by a cast aluminium body and neck, but in particular equipped with an electromagnetic pick-up with two horse-shoe shaped magnets. Around the same time, Rowe-De Armond began to produce some pick-ups for guitars, while the Dopera brothers (Dobro) supplied, a few resonator guitars with a pick-up, as early as 1932.

In 1933, Walter Fuller joined the Gibson ranks and, after several months spent in the different departments of the factory, Guy Hart asked him if he would be able to "electrify" a guitar. Being an electronics enthusiast, Walter Fuller accepted the task offered to him.

He did find several remnants left by Lloyd Loar, in particular some electrostatic pick-ups, but, considering the defects of these rudimentary units he preferred to start from scratch and pave a "new" way.

Taking into account the level of popularity of the electric Hawaiian guitar, Gibson's first goal was to bring out a model of this type, with the understanding that the pick-up could be used later to electrify an acoustic guitar.

Walter Fuller therefore began to work in order to define a new electro magnetic pick-up bearing in mind that the principle governing such a pick-up is quite simple.

As a matter of fact, it consists of a permanent magnet and a coil of insulated copper wire. The coil is placed, either around the magnet, or around a polar mass magnetized through contact with the magnet. The pick-up is then placed in such a way that a magnetic field is created around the strings, the vibrations of which generate a weak current in the coil, that can be amplified and transmitted to a loudspeaker.

The characteristics of such a pick-up vary principally in terms of :

— the gauge of the wire used in the coil
— the number of revolutions in the coil
— the type and power of the magnet
— the position of the various components.

Consequently, Walter Fuller experimented with the different combinations of these variables in order to obtain results "satisfying to the ear". The trial period covered the major part of 1934 then, at the end of that year, the prototype of the first electric Hawaiian guitar was perfected. The first samples were probably delivered starting in 1935. Indeed, it must be pointed out that no electric instruments appeared in the "W" catalog of 1934. Two versions were rather quickly offered to the public, respectively called the EH-150 and EH-100, with six or seven strings. The accompanying amplifiers of these Hawaiian guitars were specially made for Gibson by Lyon and Healy.

The pick-up used on the Hawaiian guitars was, a little later, installed in a slightly different version, on an acoustic guitar to make it the first "real" electric guitar, if one takes into consideration that the above mentioned Hawaiian guitars are a rather special category of guitar.

Gibson, in the event, drew its inspiration from a "bottom-of-the-line" model, the L-50 to be exact, which had nevertheless a solid carved top made of spruce. In fact, the L-50 has just been modified, like the majority of Gibson's acoustic models, receiving, officially on October 1, 1935, a larger body of the "Grand Auditorium" size, that is to say 16 1/4" wide by 20 1/4" long, instead of the original 14 3/4" by 19 1/4".

Several new models such as the Super 400, the L-30 or the L-37 were introduced by Gibson in 1935 and, except for the L-4, all of the existing guitars were given an enlarged body. The L-5, L-12, L-10 and L-7 went from 16" × 20" to 17" × 21" (Advanced Model), while the L-75 and L-50 grew from 14 3/4" × 19 1/4" to 16 1/4" × 20 1/4".

# THE ES-150 MODEL

The ES-150 model (ES : Electric Spanish) — in other words the electrified version of the L-50 — appeared for the first time, like the EH-150 and the EH-100, in the "X" catalog of 1936, and it began to be delivered the same year. It is, however, possible that a small number could have been produced starting at the end of 1935. We, however, believe that the first ES-150 models were marketed only in 1936.

The ES-150 model was endowed with a solid spruce top, which appears a little thicker in the middle than the one on the L-50, in order to support the mounting of the pick-up. Two very tapered "F" holes were cut on the top, while the flat back and rims were made of maple. The one-piece mahogany neck showed a triangular section (or "V" neck) typical for the period, and joined the body at the fourteenth fret. The rosewood fingerboard included nineteen frets for a 24 3/4" scale length and the bridge was made of ebony. Just like on the acoustic models of this period, the bridge was only adjustable in height with the aid of two serrated wheels located at each end, and it did not allow the intonation to be set up string by string.

From a structural point of view, the ES-150 top was reinforced with an "X-shaped" bracing while the fingerboard was firmly attached to the top in order to increase the rigidity.

The pick-up — that we will examine in details later — was mounted near the finger board, with the out-put jack located at the bottom of the tailpiece, just as on the first ever Gibson electric guitar of the 1920's we have previously examined.

The guitar was set up with a volume and a tone control acting as a treble filter, whilst the original knobs were made of brown bakelite. The top sported an elongated triangular scratch-plate, characteristic of the pre-War Gibson models.

The only available finish was "Chocolate Brown" with a golden "sunburst" on the top only.

When it was introduced in 1936, the ES-150 cost $ 72.50.

The pick-up designed by Walter Fuller and used on the first Gibson electrics quickly became known as the bar pick-up, because it had a "bar" as the polar mass. Around this bar — or rather "blade" — Walter Fuller had placed the coil, while the two magnets were set, perpendicular to the blade, and parallel to the strings. Naturally the bar pick-up, by its structure, did not have poles that could be adjusted string by string.

The different photographs allow the bulky appearance of this pick-up to be better appreciated as well as the particularity of its mounting, namely the three screws on top of the guitar. Besides, it must be pointed out that, considering its bulk, it is difficult to fit two bar pick-ups on the same guitar, unless the mounting or the size of the magnets are modified.

Under the then existing methods of research on pick-ups — we must not forget that at the time the subject was relatively new — Gibson tried various combinations and, considering the modifications that took place up

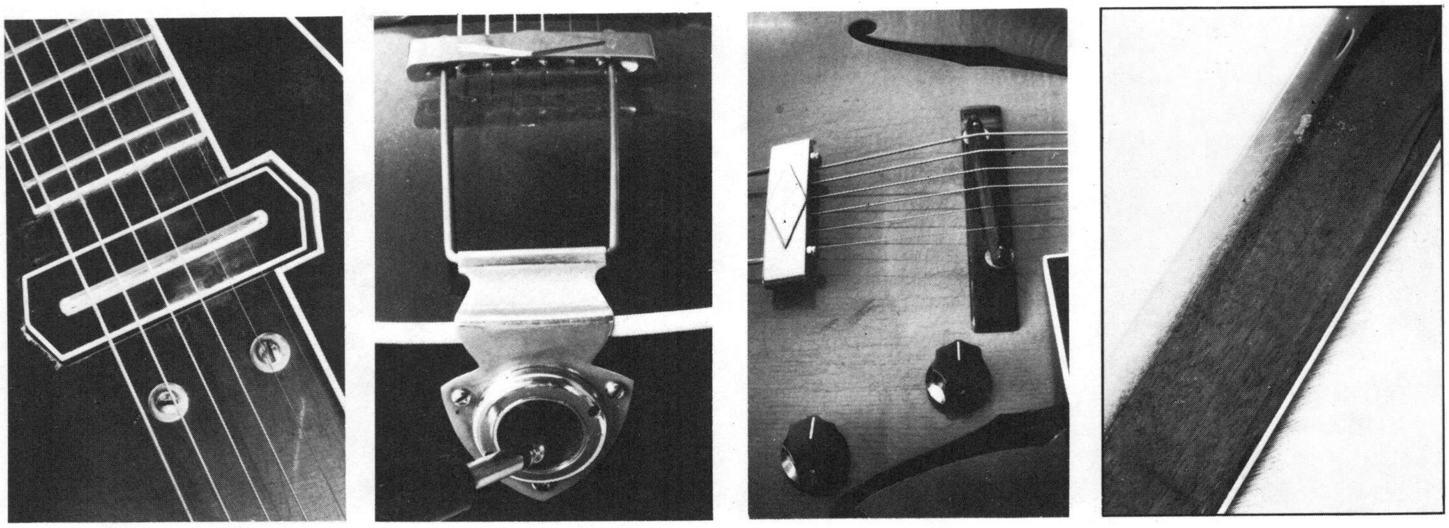

The ES-150 in details. From left to right : the bar pick-up ;
the jack output located at the base of the tailpiece ; the volume and tone controls
and the solid ebony bridge ; the triangular shape of the neck
(on this model the knobs are not original).

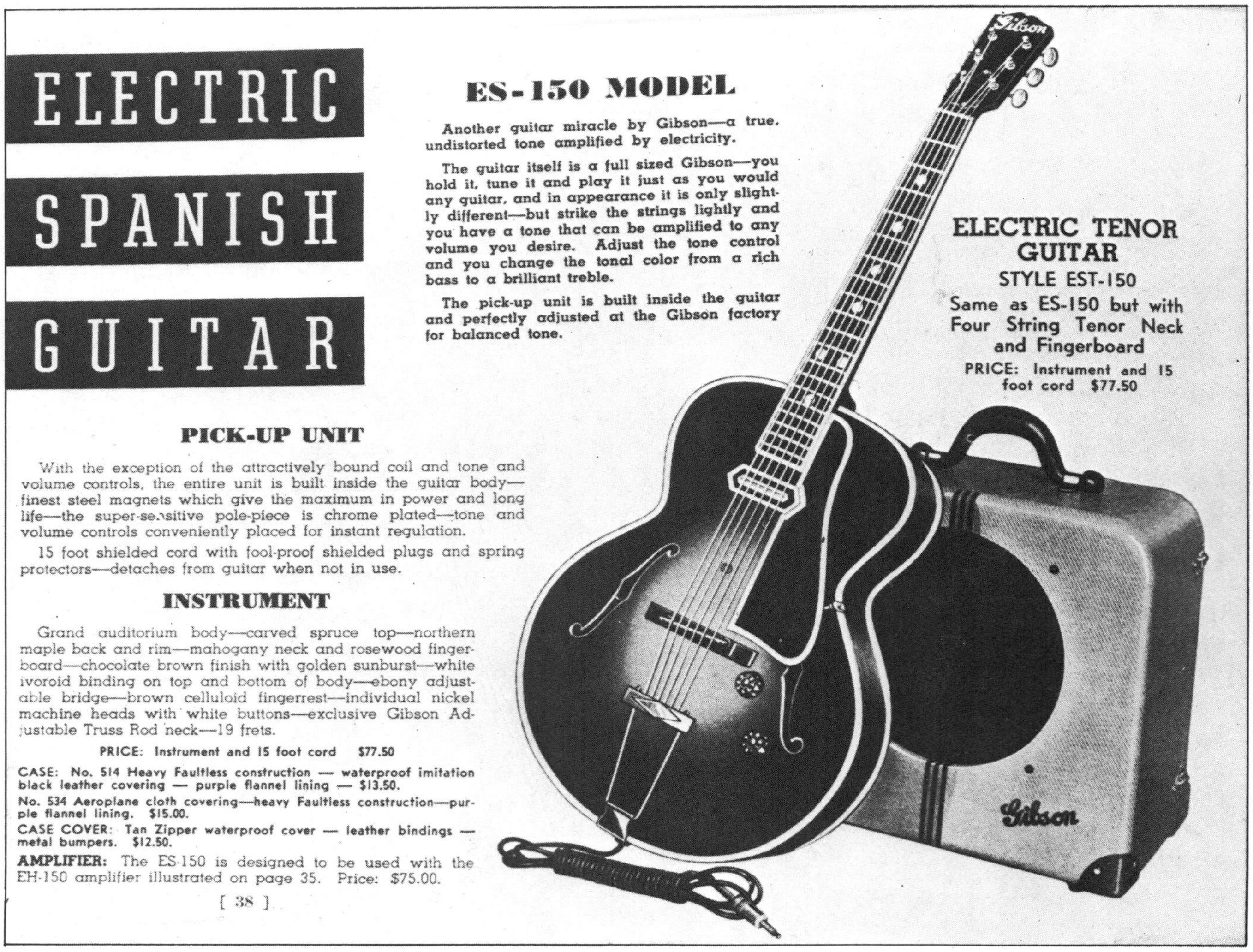

ELECTRIC

SPANISH

GUITAR

**ES-150 MODEL**

Another guitar miracle by Gibson—a true, undistorted tone amplified by electricity.

The guitar itself is a full sized Gibson—you hold it, tune it and play it just as you would any guitar, and in appearance it is only slightly different—but strike the strings lightly and you have a tone that can be amplified to any volume you desire. Adjust the tone control and you change the tonal color from a rich bass to a brilliant treble.

The pick-up unit is built inside the guitar and perfectly adjusted at the Gibson factory for balanced tone.

**ELECTRIC TENOR GUITAR**

STYLE EST-150

Same as ES-150 but with Four String Tenor Neck and Fingerboard

PRICE: Instrument and 15 foot cord $77.50

**PICK-UP UNIT**

With the exception of the attractively bound coil and tone and volume controls, the entire unit is built inside the guitar body—finest steel magnets which give the maximum in power and long life—the super-sensitive pole-piece is chrome plated—tone and volume controls conveniently placed for instant regulation.

15 foot shielded cord with fool-proof shielded plugs and spring protectors—detaches from guitar when not in use.

**INSTRUMENT**

Grand auditorium body—carved spruce top—northern maple back and rim—mahogany neck and rosewood fingerboard—chocolate brown finish with golden sunburst—white ivoroid binding on top and bottom of body—ebony adjustable bridge—brown celluloid fingerrest—individual nickel machine heads with white buttons—exclusive Gibson Adjustable Truss Rod neck—19 frets.

PRICE: Instrument and 15 foot cord $77.50

CASE: No. 514 Heavy Faultless construction — waterproof imitation black leather covering — purple flannel lining — $13.50.

No. 534 Aeroplane cloth covering—heavy Faultless construction—purple flannel lining. $15.00.

CASE COVER: Tan Zipper waterproof cover — leather bindings — metal bumpers. $12.50.

**AMPLIFIER:** The ES-150 is designed to be used with the EH-150 amplifier illustrated on page 35. Price: $75.00.

[ 38 ]

Excerpt from the "Y" catalog of 1937 depicting the Es-150 model.

The famed "bar" pick-up designed by Walter Fuller around 1934. This picture clearly evidences the length of the two magnets as well as the way the unit is affixed to the top of the guitar.

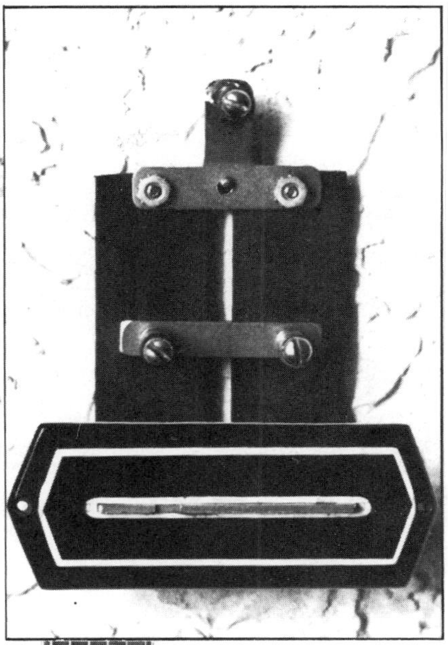

Jimmy Raney with an ES-150 in the early fifties.

The ES-150 body with its tapered "F" holes.

The great pioneer of the electric guitar... Charlie Christian (1919-1942).

until around 1938, there are at least three slightly different types of bar pick-ups.

As regards magnets, Walter Fuller told us that a nickel-base magnet was initially used on the first models, before being replaced by a cobalt-base magnet. In addition, these subsequent magnets were at first composed of 17 % cobalt and then finally of 36 % cobalt.

The nickel and cobalt magnets can easily be told apart by the naked eye thanks to their color, as the nickel magnet is light silver while the cobalt one is dark blue, almost black.

The coil was also modified as the first pick-ups had 4,000 turns of number 38 wire, before changing, a little later, to 10,000 turns of number 42 wire (0.0025" thick) in other words, a greater number of turns of a thinner wire, in order to have a higher impedance.

The position of the pick-up was adjustable with the aid of the three visible screws and a certain variation in the tone could be obtained according to the placement.

Also to be noted is that on all the first models the cross bar between the coil and the magnet was higher than on the later models.

Lacking adjustable poles, the pick-up blade did not allow the volume of each string to be properly set up, and very quickly a number of guitarists made notches in this blade — mostly in the B-noté region — in order to lower somewhat the volume of certain strings and improve the overall balance.

The ES-150 did not meet with a spectacular success, and generally speaking the electric guitar will not really "take off" until just after the Second World War. However, one man was to contribute more than any other to immortalizing this model, that is still associated with his name. We are speaking of Charlie Christian.

After meeting Eddie Durham in 1937 when he was eighteen years old, Charlie Christian became very interested in the electric guitar, whose potential he very quickly realized. In 1939, thanks to John Hammond, he was auditioned by Benny Goodman, who signed him up after hearing him play a few bars. From that date on, he could finally show what a guitar player was capable of, by developing, a little like a tenor saxophone, the linear idea of the chorus.

Surely, considering the level of the media in 1940, there is no doubt that the Charlie Christian phenomenon did not spread as it would have in today's conditions. Nevertheless, he is of great importance as the forerunner of the modern guitar, because even if he was no the first to make use of it, it was Charlie Christian who revealed the possibilities of the electric guitar.

Unfortunately, an attack of tuberculosis in the summer of 1941 greatly shortened his career, and Charlie Christian died in March 1942 at the age of 23.

The ES-150 and especially the bar pick-up, serve as witnesses of his influence, as both are commonly nicknamed "Charlie Christian" models.

Later on, the ES-150 model with a bar pick-up was equally adopted by influential jazz guitarists, such as Jimmy Raney and René Thomas.

# OTHER ELECTRIC GUITARS OF THE PRE-WAR PERIOD

Besides a four-string electric "tenor" guitar called the EST-150, Gibson had, also introduced in its "Z" catalog of 1938, a second electric model under the name ES-100.

Whereas the ES-150 took its inspiration from the L-50, the ES-100 was clearly derived from the L-30, whose general characteristics it followed, with, in addition, a bar pick-up having a 17 % cobalt magnet (and not 36 % like the ES-150 of that period).

It was supposed to be the "economy" model of the electric line... an ever present idea at Gibson.

Besides having a smaller body than the ES-150 (14 3/4" × 19 1/4"), the ES-100 was characterized by a lateral out-put jack instead of one at the tailpiece base. The coil of the pick-up was rectangular and white, and not black with a white binding as on the 150 model.

Despite being an inexpensive model the top was made of spruce, while the flat bottom and the rims were of maple. The single-piece neck was of mahogany, and the fingerboard, as well as the bridge, were of rosewood. The

Gibson

The ES-250 as it appeared in the "AA" catalog of 1940

The small size ES-100 introduced in 1938

Gibson

After the bar-pick-up was withdrawn in 1940, the ES-150 was fitted with a new single coil unit located near the bridge.

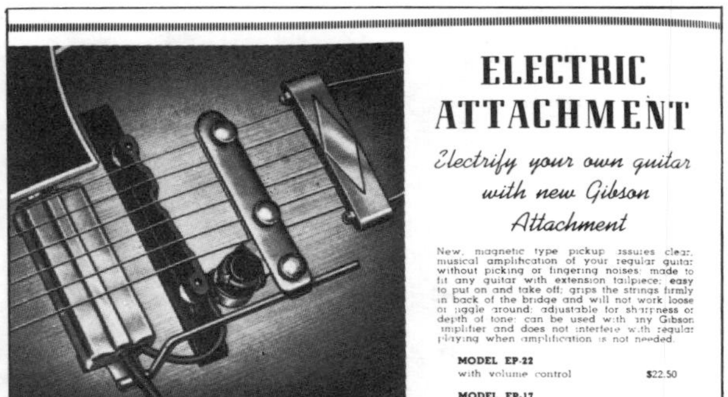
ELECTRIC
ATTACHMENT
Electrify your own guitar with new Gibson Attachment
New, magnetic type pickup assures clear, musical amplification of your regular guitar without picking or fingering noises; made to fit any guitar with extension tailpiece; easy to put on and take off; grips the strings firmly in back of the bridge and will not work loose or jiggle around; adjustable for sharpness or depth of tone; can be used with any Gibson amplifier and does not interfere with regular playing when amplification is not needed.
MODEL EP-22
with volume control $22.50
MODEL EP-17
without volume control 17.50

Besides its range of electrics,
Gibson also commercialized two pick-up units – respectively designated EP-22 and EP-17 – which could be adapted to any arched-top guitar.

The ES-125 was first introduced in 1941 to replace the ES-100.

fingerboard offered 19 frets for a scale length of 24 3/4". The ES-100 was only available in "Chocolate Brown" with a golden sunburst on top.

On the price list dated October 25, 1939, the ES-150 cost $ 85.25, while the ES-100 went for $ 53.90.

In the "AA" catalog of 1940, no less than nine pages (of a special yellowed color) were devoted to electric models, among them 4 Hawaiian guitars : the EH-185, EH-150, EH-100 and the Grand Console ; 2 mandolins : EM-150 and EM-100 ; one tenor banjo : EMS-150 ; and three guitars.

Besides the ES-150 and ES-100, Gibson had just added a new model designated the ES-250, this time, as a "top of the line" based upon an L-7 type (advanced model) guitar, with a 17" × 21" body.

Except for a naturally more luxurious ornamentation with fine bindings and inlays on the fingerboard, the ES-250 kept to the pattern of the time with a solid carved top made of spruce, and maple carved back and rims. The neck was of mahogany while the fingerboard and bridge were of rosewood. Considering the dimensions of the model, the scale length was 25 1/2" instead of 24 3/4", but the neck-to-body junction was as usual at the fourteenth fret.

The ES-250 was equipped with a bar pick-up, a volume control, a tone control, and like the ES-150, the out-put jack was placed at the base of the tailpiece. In fact, the ES-250 was only manufactured during approximately a year, and that is why today one of these guitars is quite rare, although the exact shipping total is not ascertained.

On October 1, 1940, Gibson published a supplement to its "AA" catalog, noticeably changing the line of electric instruments, and in particular, the three guitars marketed up to that time, namely the ES-150, ES-100 and ES-250.

The most striking feature of this supplement was the disappearance of the bar pick-up.

The sheer reasons for its abandon are not officially known but, if the usual Gibson policy is any indication, we can believe that the bar pick-up was simply replaced by a pick-up that Gibson's ever-continuous research had proven to be superior.

It is, however, to be noted that if Gibson dropped the bar pick-up from its stock models, it was practically always possible for a guitarist to have one mounted on his guitar "on a special order" basis. Indeed, the Gibson factory always kept at its disposal the parts needed for their assembly. In the 1940's, 1950's and even 1960's, a certain number of acoustic models such as L-5's or L-7's were thus "electrified" with a bar pick-up, even when this was no longer officially proposed as an accessory. Moreover some electric models lost their original pick-up for a bar pick-up salvaged from the factory or taken apart from an older model. In each case, it would not be a "stock" model, but rather a unique, guitar modified by a customer or make on a special order basis by the Gibson factory.

To follow the bar pick-up, Gibson introduced two types of pick-ups : the first — that we will call the "large diagonal pick-up" — was on a new model designated the ES-300 which replaced the short lived ES-250 ; the second — rectangular — was on the new ES-150 and ES-100.

The ES-300, therefore, replaced the ES-250, but kept its main characteristics i.e. a 17" × 21" body, a solid spruce top, back and rims of curly maple, and a rosewood fingerboard. However, a certain number of differences can be noted, such as :

— a "Natural" finish instead of the Chocolate Brown Sunburst

— a maple neck (instead of mahogany)

— a 20 fret fingerboard (instead of 19) with L-7 type double parallelogram position markers

— a modified tailpiece, inspired from the L-5 model

— a lateral out-put jack, and not one at the base of the tailpiece

— and, of course, a new pick-up.

The "large diagonal pick-up", as shown in the reproduction of the 1940 catalog practically extended from the bottom part of the fingerboard to the bridge. Its height could be adjusted with the aid of two screws located at either end, and in addition, it had poles that were adjustable string-by-string, unlike the bar pick-up.

According to Walt Fuller, Gibson's objective with this pick-up was to obtain a "natural" sound, that is rather "amplified" and not

The ES-300 was first introduced in late 1940 with a large diagonal pick-up.

Close-up view of the small diagonal pick-up. Note the spruce top used on the pre-war ES-300's.

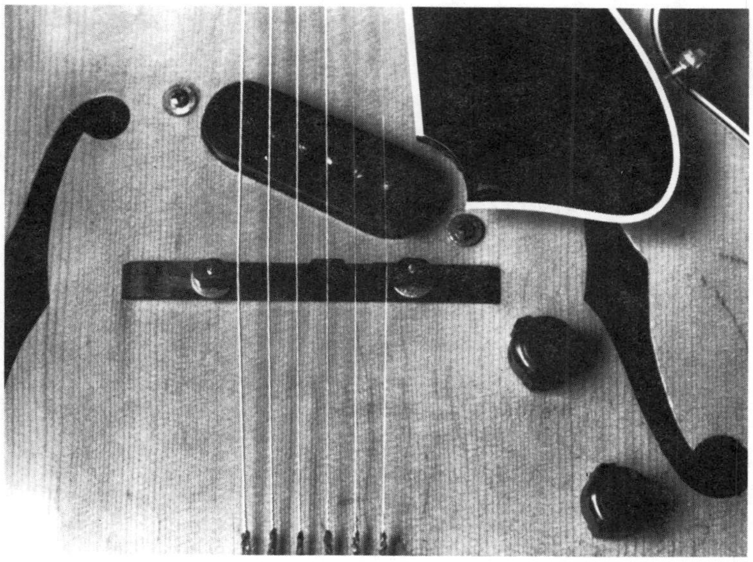

A few months after it was presented to the public, the ES-300 was modified and fitted with a "smaller" diagonal pick-up set up near the bridge.

so much electric, thus explaining its positioning on a wide register between the fingerboard and the bridge. The large diagonal pick-up had four flat and rectangular magnets of a new type : the first Alnico magnets. The name "Alnico" is applied to a magnet that, besides iron, includes aluminium, nickel and cobalt. This new single coil pick-up had theoretically 10,000 turns of number 42 wire.

The ES-300 took its name from the fact that on October 1, 1940, what Gibson announced as the "Deluxe ES-300 Outfit" — that is the guitar, its case, the EH-275 amplifier and connecting wires — cost... $ 300.00 ! The ES-300 guitar alone sold for $ 160.00.

From an aesthetic and anecdotal point of view, the ES-300 was the first electric model to have the crown shape pearl inlay on the headstock, something which afterwards was to be found on a very large number of models, and became a Gibson classic feature.

As for the ES-150 and ES-100, they were given a new rectangular shaped pick-up this time located near the bridge and not at the end of the fingerboard. This new pick-up also possessed poles that were adjustable string-by-string, but it was less powerful than the large diagonal pick-up, due to a weaker magnet. The first models were equipped with a metal cover, which was judged too capacative, and soon replaced by a plastic cover.

The ES-150, in turn, was given a lateral out-put jack which, in fact, permitted the guitar to be left upright, even when it was plugged in. Finally it must be pointed out that the ES-100 and ES-150, unlike the ES-300, were still only available in the "Chocolate Brown" sunburst finish.

On October 1, 1940, the prices of the new ES-150 and ES-100 were set as follows.
*ES-150 outfit (guitar and amplifier) :
— $ 185.000 with the EH-185 amplifier
— $ 175.00 with the EH-150 amplifier
while the ES-150 alone, cost $ 85.50.
*ES-100 Outfit (guitar and amplifier) :
— $ 127.00 With the EH-100 amplifier
while the ES-100 alone cost $ 59.00.

The type of amplifiers were christened at that time according to the electric Hawaiian guitars for which they were created : EH-275, EH-185, EH-150 and EH-100.

Then, a little after the fashion of the famous DeArmond pick up, Gibson marketed two pick-ups which could be adapted to any arched top guitar in search of electrification.

The first model designated EP-22 cost $ 22.50 on October 1, 1940, and was supplied with a volume control, while the second one designated EP-17 cost $ 17.50 and was identical to the EP-22 with no volume control.

These pick-ups did not have string-by-string adjustable poles, and were adapted to the guitar by means of a rod attached to the strings between the bridge and the tailpiece. It could, however, be adjusted at will near the fingerboard or the bridge.

Paradoxically, the large diagonal pick-up did not meet with the success anticipated by the Gibson engineers as the guitarists required then an "electric" sound, in order to benefit from the change in playing technique that the electric guitar entailed and the effects it allowed.

Therefore, at the beginning of 1941, Gibson modified the ES-300, this time giving it a "smaller diagonal pick-up" located near the bridge. Like the preceding one, the height of this diagonal pick-up was adjustable by means of two screws at either end and it had string-by-string adjustable poles. However, because of its modest dimensions, it had only two magnets but still with a 10,000 turn coil.

This new variation was announced in a second supplement to the "AA" catalog dated May 20, 1941. This supplement equally marked the change of the name from ES-100 to ES-125, without any apparent modification in the specifications of the guitar.

A few months earlier in January 1941 Gibson announced the introduction of an electric guitar in the Kalamazoo series which, since around 1930, had been offering inexpensive instruments manufactured by the company under a different trade name. This new guitar was named "KES" (Kalamazoo Electric Spanish).

It had the dimensions of an ES-100, with a spruce top and mahogany back and rims. The "KES" was equipped with a rectangular pick-up which was similar to the one on the ES-100 of that period and placed near the bridge. Its price with the amplifier was $ 97.50.

A little later, in May 1941, Gibson introduced an even more "economical" model under the name "MESG", that is : Master-

CABLE ADDRESS
"GIBMANDLIN"

Gibson

GUITARS
BANJOS
MANDOLINS
UKULELES

WESTERN UNION A. B. C.
AND BENTLEY CODES

GIBSON, INC., KALAMAZOO, MICHIGAN

Dear Gibson Dealer:

During the present War Production period, we are developing New Production Methods, New Materials, and New Ideas In Design that will give you BETTER Gibson Instruments than ever before.

In the meantime, we want to make as many of the more popular models as restrictions and available man power will permit so you will have a fair assortment to offer your friends and customers. A limited number of the following models will be available this Fall and Winter:

| | |
|---|---|
| L-00 Flat Top | $36.75 |
| 115 Challenge case | 6.75 |
| LG-2 Flat Top | 42.50 |
| 117 Challenge case | 6.75 |
| J-45 Jumbo | 50.00 |
| 118 Challenge case | 7.25 |
| Southerner-Jumbo | 94.50 |
| 514 Faultless case | 19.75 |
| L-50 Carved Top | 68.25 |
| 103 Challenge case | 7.25 |
| 514 Faultless case | 19.75 |
| L-7 Carved Top | 131.25 |
| 606 Faultless case | 25.00 |
| 600 Faultless case | 32.50 |

Prices include Federal Excise Tax--All models are with regular Sunburst Finish.

For the first few months production will be on a very small scale because at least 90% of our employees will remain on War Production work. On your first order we will be forced to limit each dealer to ONE of EACH MODEL. Later, if additional men are available, production will be increased. We cannot guarantee delivery of all items, and no definite delivery dates can be given.

Metal truss rods will be eliminated, but each neck will be reinforced with hard wood for additional strength. A substitute will be used for the metal bar on extension tailpieces for carved guitars. Machine heads on all guitars will be "three on a plate" and of the best quality obtainable. Kalamazoo instruments will be discontinued for the duration.

Sincerely,

GIBSON, INC.

GIBSON ELECTRICAL INSTRUMENTS . . GIBSON MONA STEEL STRINGS

During the second World War, Gibson sent a copy of this letter to its dealers to inform them of the models available from the factory.

*"25" The ES-150, affectionately known as the "Charlie Christian model." Note on the front view, the width of the fingerboard as well as the slender shape of the "F" holes. The triangular profile of the neck is clearly evidenced on the back view. Unfortunately this instrument does not have the original tuning gears and control knobs.*

*"26" — **Left :** ES-300 (1941) with spruce top and small diagonal pick-up.*
*— **Right :** ES-300 (1951) with laminated maple top and two P-90's. Note the master tone control on the upper bout.*

*"27" The ES-125 in its first post-War edition with pearloid "crown" position markers. On this model the single coil pick-up does not have adjustable pole pieces.*

*"28" — **Left :** The ES-175 as it was introduced in 1949 with one p.u. and a 19 fret fingerboard.*
*— **Right :** ES-350 (1950) with two single coil pick-ups and 3 controls.*

*"29" ES-5 N (1951).*
*Introduced in 1949 as "the supreme electronic version of the famed L-5", the ES-5 was in all probability the first electric guitar fitted with 3 pick-ups. On this model the original tuning gears have been replaced by Grover Imperial Keys.*

*"30" A close-up view of an L-5 CES (1957) equipped with two Alnico pick-ups. Each oblong pole piece is actually a magnet adjustable in height thanks to the small screws located in the holes on the cover.*

*"31" ES-350 (1955) with the standard Gibson wiring featuring dual volume and tone controls for each pick-up and a 3 position toggle switch.*
*On this example the original tailpiece has been unfortunately replaced. The original part is similar to the one fitted on the 3-control ES-350.*

*"32" SUPER 400 CES (1957).*
*Note the Tune-O-Matic instead of the rosewood compensating bridge featured on the other models of this gallery.*

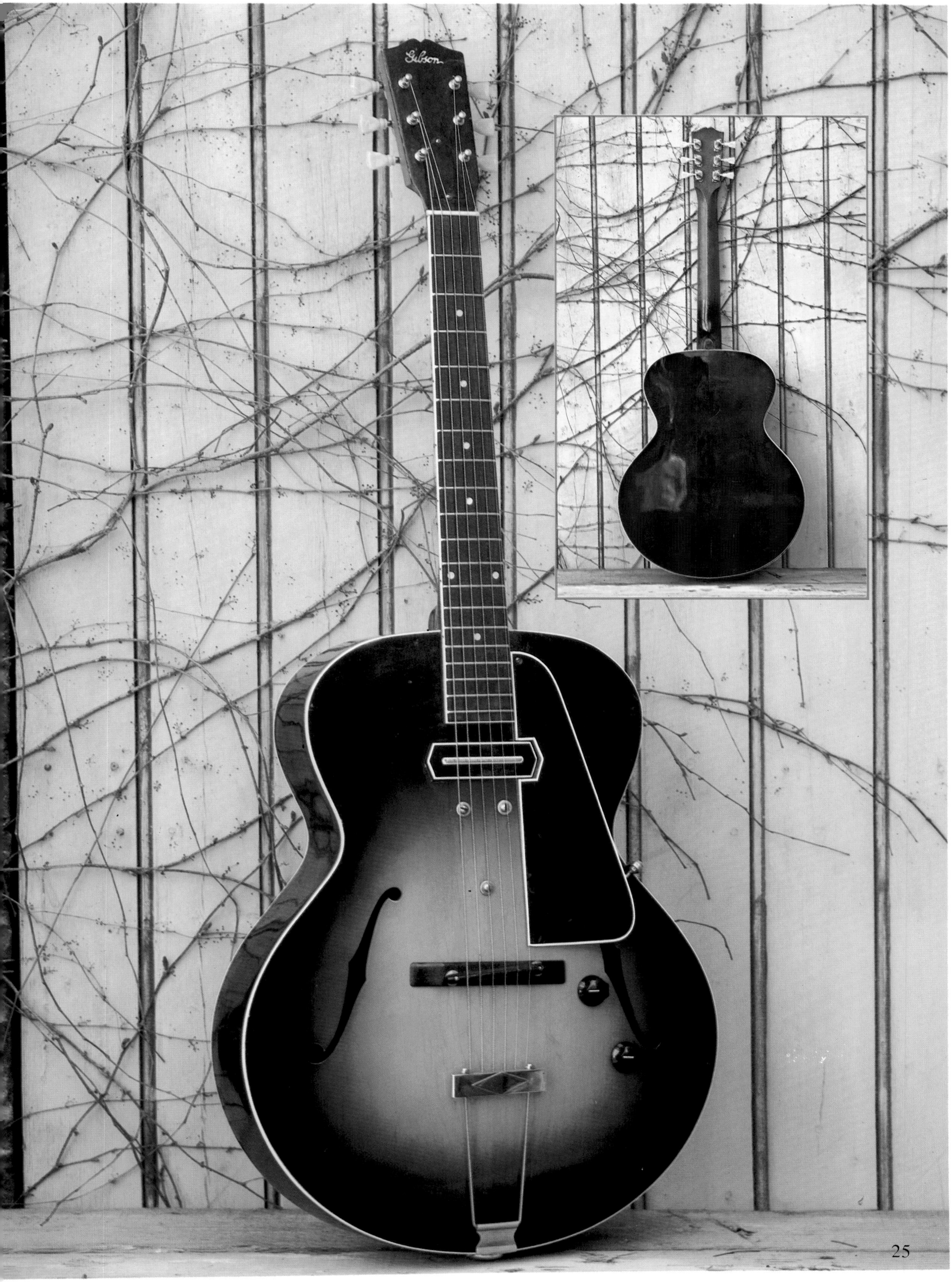
Gibson

Gibson

Gibson

tone Electric Spanish Guitar. With a price of $ 65.00 with amplifier, the "MESG" was made entirely of mahogany and equipped with a rectangular pick-up without adjustable poles.

The goal of these two Gibson attempts—even though they did not directly carry the Gibson name — was to make the electric guitar more affordable to a larger number of people.

The "BB" catalog of 1942 was the last of the "pre-War" period and it confirmed the changes that took place in 1941, with the exception that the ES-300 was available either with a regular finish (that is "Chocolate Brown Sunburst"), at the price of $ 173.25 or with a Natural (or blonde) finish for $ 183.75.

# THE OUT-BREAK OF WAR

The events that took place in the world prompted production manager Wallace B. Caldwell to write the following words to one of the Gibson dealers as early as July 1941 :

*"At present our supply of material is spotty... things such as amplifiers, magnets and other electrical parts, we do not know from day to day when we will get more, when the present supply is exhausted".*

The attack on Pearl Harbor on December 7, 1941 did not improve this situation, as the entry of the United States into war meant for Gibson, as it did for all companies, restrictions on critical materials. The U.S. goverment limitation orders quickly forced the Gibson company to stop the manufacture of musical instruments and with supplies already difficult in 1941, regular production was suspended at the beginning of 1942.

Gibson was then, along with 90 % of its staff, integrated into the war effort and, considering its highly qualified workmanship was especially used in the sub-contracting of mechanical and electrical components.

Only a few employees continued to work on the last floor of the building at 225 Parsons Street, in order to service Gibson products and complete the assembly of the different units under process... A certain number of instruments were, however manufactured during the War with parts held in stock and Gibson sent a letter to its dealers stipulating which models were available. Until further notice, each dealer could order only one guitar.

Of course, because of the restrictions on materials such as metals there were no electric guitars among the instruments made or rather assembled, during the Second World War.

It is, nevertheless, interesting to note the guitars Gibson could supply :

— the L-00 and LG-2, "Flat Top" guitars, the J-45 and SJ, Jumbo "Flat Top" guitars, and finally, the L-50 and L-7, carved top "F" holes guitars.

The models released during this period are characterized by a truss rod made of hardwood instead of metal. Also, in order to save as much metal as possible, the string retainer of the tailpiece was equally made of wood.

The last electric guitars of the "pre-War" period were undoubtedly finished in the very early stages of 1942 and normal production in Kalamazoo did not resume until four years later.

# CHAPTER 2

# THE POST-WAR PERIOD
# THE RISE OF THE ELECTRIC GUITAR

As the second World War terminated the production of musical instruments started again at Gibson around the end of 1945. However, the normal production rhythm of the factory did not really take up again until the first months of 1946.

In 1944 the Chicago Musical Instruments company acquired a controlling interest in Gibson Inc. and anticipated that the demand for fretted instruments at the end of the War would quite exceed the previous production capabilities.

Thus, in response to the great needs of a market that had been "frustrated" for nearly four years, Gibson, on resuming its activities, inaugurated a new millroom as well as an enlarged lumber storage area. These additions to the 1917 premises had been built in 1945, and with the return to normal activity, they proved to be most useful in helping Gibson to satisfy a demand unprecedented in its history. As a matter of fact, such a flow of orders for the various instruments of the Gibson line had never been received before.

In spite of the War, and the slow- down it had imposed on the evolution of the instruments, the electric guitar had unquestionably progressed and a strong demand for this type of instrument appeared. Of course, right after the War, the Hawaiian guitar still held a certain supremacy, but the adoption of the electric guitar by several jazz and blues musicians, not to mention all the amateur guitarists gave the instrument a stimulus that since has not stopped.

As regards jazz, "Be-Bop" replaced "Swing" and Charlie Christian, Oscar Moore and George Barnes were followed by Barney Kessel and Tal Farlow. Little by little, the blues was also converted to "electrics" thanks to Mr. T. Bone Walker and his bar pick-up ES-300, and then Muddy Waters and Elmore James. Naturally, most of these musicians played on Gibson guitars and their success, without a doubt, contributed to promote a line that had been continually expanding over the years.

## THE ES-300, ES-150 AND ES-125 MODELS

In 1946, besides various Hawaiian guitars and mandolins, Gibson offered three models of "Electric Spanish" guitars. Barnes Reinecke's new "Ultratone" Hawaiian guitar was still making the cover of the first post-War electric catalog, but Gibson had not remained inactive during War time, as the three models in question, the **ES-300, ES-150** and the **ES-125,** had been slightly modified compared to their 1942 specifications.

* The **ES-300,** still 17" × 21", was above all characterized by its new single coil pick-up, now located at the end of the fingerboard.

The diagonal pick-up, placed near the bridge, had in turn been dropped, undoubtedly because of its sharp and agressive sonority, and replaced by a rectangular-shaped pick-up with two "ears" on either side to attach it to the top of the guitar. This new pick-up had two flat rectangular Alnico (II or IV) type magnets with a coil of 10,000 turns of number 42 wire, and the poles corresponding to each string were adjustable. Naturally,

A post War ES-300 with laminated maple top and a single coil pick-up near the fingerboard.

After WW II the ES-150 was enlarged with a 17'' wide body similar to the ES-300. This is the early fifties edition with trapezoidal position markers.

A 1948 ES-125, with its unbound fingerboard and "crown" markers.

The single coil pick-up used on the ES-125 right after the war was characterized by its non adjustable pole pieces.

the new position of the pick-up gave the instrument a mellower (and "jazzier") tone than the diagonal pick-up of the former edition. This new single coil pick-up was destined to set the pace in its category for the next two or three decades under the code name P.U. 90 or P. 90 as it is often called.

Unlike most pre-War models, the new ES-300 did not have a solid spruce top, but a laminated maple top. Gibson undoubtedly realized how little influence a solid top had on the quality of an electric sound, which is produced by the vibration of the string, more than the vibration of the top.

Besides it appears that several jazz players — such as Tal Farlow — preferred a laminated top to a solid one as it generated less vibration. Thus the guitar had a less brilliant tone, more appropriate to the sound they were after, in order to match their style.

In another respect, like on all the post-War electric acoustic guitars, the bracing consisted of a pair of lengthwise bars with sometimes an additional reinforcement on certain models (ex. : Super 400). The "X"-shaped bracing (or cross bracing) used before the War was not applied to an electric guitar until much later on a model like the Johnny Smith.

Equally to be noted on the first post-War ES-300 is a new tailpiece, on which two small "F"-holes were cut out to remind those on top. Like before, the ES-300 was available in the normal "sunburst" finish (golden sunburst on top and back of the instrument) and for a small extra charge in a "natural" (or Blonde) finish.

* The **ES-150** was even more drastically modified, as it dropped the 16 1/4" × 20 1/4" body — of the L-50 — to come into line with an "Advanced Size" body like the ES-300, that is to say, 17" × 21", with a 20 fret-fingerboard instead of 19.

The pick-up was practically identical to the one on the ES-300 and located, as well, at the end of the fingerboard, for a mellower sound. The fingerboard had small pearl dot position markers and the only finish avalaible was the traditional "Chocolate Brown" with a golden sunburst on top.

*The **ES-125** equally took on some volume going from 14 3/4" × 19 1/4" to the dimensions formerly used by the ES-150, that is 16 1/4" × 20 1/4". The rosewood fingerboard still had 19 frets and a 24 3/4" scale length. The pick-up was different from the one mounted on the ES-300 or the ES-150, as it did not have adjustable pole pieces, but 6 direct Alnico magnets which gave it a "punchier" sound with a lot of attack.

To our knowledge this very peculiar pick-up (see color photograph) was not widely used on other Gibson electrics despite its noticeable sound and it remained distinctive on the early post-War ES-125. At the beginning of the fifties a regular P 90 with adjustable poles pieces was adopted.

On the first issue ES-125 the unbound fingerboard had somewhat paradoxically trapazoidal (or crown) position markers and not pearl dots, as on the ES-150. "Sunburst" was the only available finish.

Looking at these three models, one can easily see, the distinct evolution followed by Gibson with the single pick-up then in use shifted from the bridge to the end of the fingerboard. The increase in the volume of the bodies of the 150 and 125 is also of interest, as well as the disappearance of solid carved tops which clearly evidenced the emphasis on an electric sound as apposed to a purely amplified sound.

# THE ES-350 MODEL

These three guitars were completed in 1947 by a new model designated **ES-350** which, in fact, proved to be an ES-300 with a rounded Venitian cutaway. The evolution was fairly logical and Gibson, in bringing out its first electric guitar with a cutaway, under the name ES-350 "Premier", was taking up the designation used, beginning in 1939, for the cutaway "Super 400 and "L-5".

The ES-350, on which among others, Talmadge (Tal) Farlow was to make himself famous during the 1950' had general specifications identical to those of the ES-300. It was made entirely of maple, often with a gentle curl, with a laminated maple neck and a rosewood fingerboard. Like the ES-300, the ES-350 had "double parallelogram" position markers and the peg head was inlaid with the Gibson "crown". The tailpiece with two "F" holes featured the first Post-War ES-300 gave

The original ES-350 with only one pick-up. Note the pre-War logo inlaid on the headstock.

TAL FARLOW

Barney Kessel
with his modified ES-350.

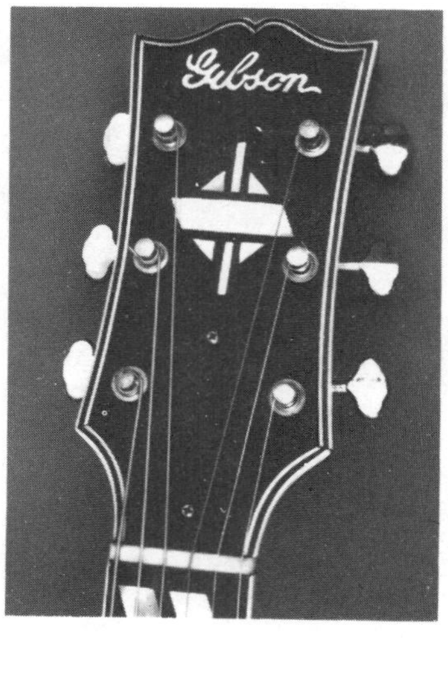


The "old" Gibson logo – often called "pre-War" logo – used until 1948...

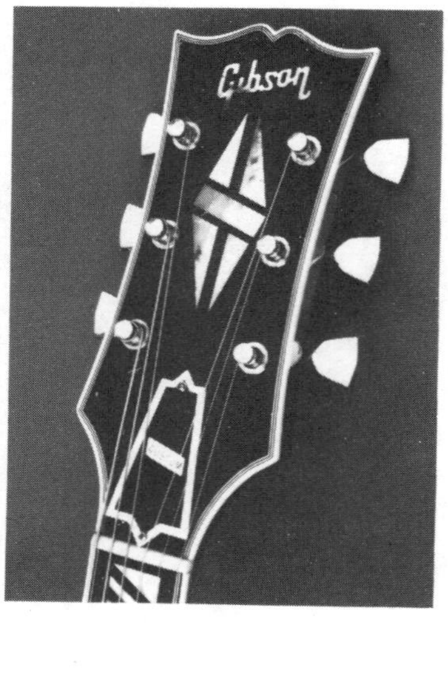


...and the current logo introduced in 1948.

place to a more traditional trapeze tailpiece with pointed extremities.

In the leaflet introducing the ES-350, Gibson stipulated that the pick-up had Alnico V magnets, whereas they were most certainly Alnico IV or even Alnico II, actually a little weaker magnet. If anything, magnets have considerably evolved over the years and can be a source of discrepancies by today's standards.

The first version of the ES-350 had only one pick-up located at the end of the fingerboard, and it was not until 1948 that both the ES-350 and ES-300 were stock equipped with two pick-ups and three controls.

Finally the change in the style of the "Gibson" logo inlaid on the peg head of the guitars came about progressively beginning in 1948. However the first issue ES-350 models have a "pre-War" logo.

The Gibson price list drawn up on December 1, 1947, offered the following electric guitars :

- ES-350 Premier :
  $ 325.00 with a "Sunburst" finish ;
  $ 340.00 with a "Natural" finish ;
- ES-300 :
  $ 225.00 with a "Sunburst" finish ;
  $ 240.00 with a "Natural" finish
- ES-150 :
  $ 147.50 with a "Sunburst" finish ;
- ES-125 :
  $ 97.50 with a "Sunburst" finish ;

It must be pointed out however that no electric guitar at that time reached the price of the Super 400 when it was introduced in 1935 that is $ 400.00.

# TED MAC CARTY'S BEGINNINGS

In march of 1948, Theodore M. MacCarty joined the Gibson ranks where he was to stay for eighteen years and enjoy a highly successful career, first as Vice President and General Manager during 1948 at 1949, then as President and General Manager starting in 1950.

Theodore M. MacCarty, on the very first year of his association with Gibson, perfected a fingerrest pick-up adaptable to all arched top acoustic guitars. (Patent number 2,567,570 registered on November 2, 1948.) The idea was quite simple and very ingenious, as it consisted of attaching a pick-up to a scratch plate, which could then be placed on practically any guitar to "electrify" it. This fingerrest unit, whose pick-up was especially flat, was available in a one or two-pick-up version with volume and tone controls.

At this stage, without creating a large range of electrics, Gibson could convert most of the acoustic models into electric thus enabling the customers to choose for example, a more luxurious carved top model such as the Super 400, the L-5 or the L-12.

The system advantageously replaced the EP-22 and EP-17 units, introduced before the War, and the guitar could keep all its acoustic properties. Last but not least, it was easy to make the conversion at any time, avoiding regrets to the guitarist who might have drilled out impetuously the top of his guitar in order to fit it out with a pick-up... before changing his mind, once the damage done !

The fingerrest pick-ups were listed for the first time in the Gibson catalog at the end of 1948 as an accessory, but in order to outline their use even better, a special model was also introduced in 1948 under the name "**L-7E**" and "**L-7PE**". It was simply a stock L-7, on which the unit designed by Ted MacCarty was mounted at the factory.

The "L-7E" (E : Electric) was the version without a cutaway, while the "L-7PE" (P : Premier, E : Electric) had a rounded Venetian cutaway. A double-pick-up unit was even offered for each model respectively as "**L-7ED**" (Electric Double) and "**L-7PED**" (Premier Electric Double) ; but they were available only starting in 1949.

The basic finish of the "electrified" L-7's was initially (and only) the traditional sunburst, but in 1950, a "natural" option was also offered for each model, until it their discontinuation in 1954.

In 1949, the name "Premier" was discarded and to indicate the presence of a cutaway on a model available with or without one, Gibson henceforth used the word "Cutaway".

The "L-7PE" and "L-7PED" thus became respectively the "**L-7CE**" and the "**L-7CED**".

In 1948, as already mentioned Gibson modified the ES-300 and ES-350, to supply both of them, with two pick-ups instead of one,

ES-300 (1951)
This is the last version with two pick-ups and three controls. The model was officially discontinued in 1952.

ES-350 (1950)
Around 1948 the 350 was fitted with two single coil pick-ups and three controls.

L-7 CE

The fingerrest unit perfected by Ted MacCarty in 1948 was available either with one or two pick-ups. It was supplied with volume and tone controls, but the pick-ups did not have adjustable pole pieces.

The SUPER 400 headstock with its remarkable split diamond inlay.

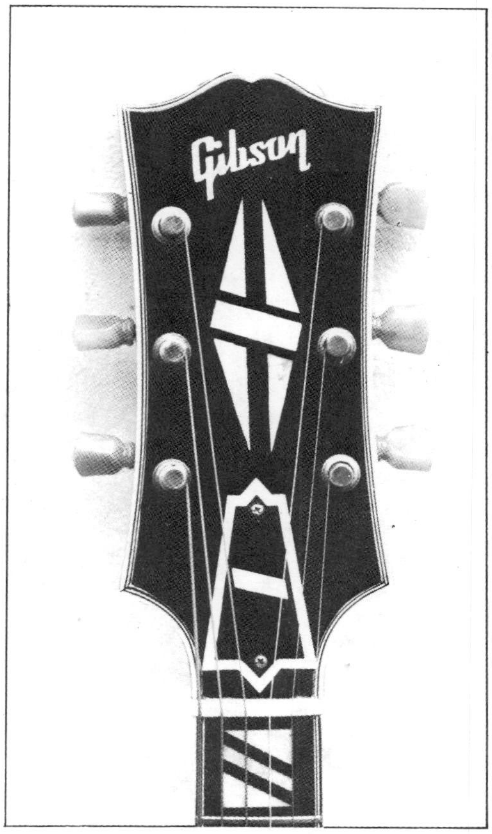

1949 SUPER 400 factory equipped with a fingerrest pick-up unit. Note curly maple back.

in order to obtain a much wider variation of sounds. However, the ES-300 and ES-300 models did not yet have the classic three-position toggle switch, but two volume controls (one for each pick-up) acting as mixers and strategically placed near the bridge while a master tone control mounted near the cutaway bout complemented the tonal possibilities.

It is not until around 1952 that the ES-350 was finally equipped with independent volume and tone controls for each pick-up, as well as a 3-position toggle switch located on the upper bout near the Venetian cutaway.

As for the ES-300, it was discontinued in 1952 — it did not appear in the Gibson catalog of that year — and it was never equipped in all probability with a 3-position toggle switch. At least, we have never came across such a model and the last ES-300's were shipped in 1953, undoubtedly with their 3 control circuitry.

Gibson was to persue the expansion of its line on the threshold of the 1950's, introducing two new particularly striking models namely the ES-175 and the ES-5.

# THE ES-175 AND ES-5 MODELS

More than thirty years after its presentation the **ES-175** has become such a "classic" of its kind, that it is practically superfluous to introduce it to a jazz guitarist. We no longer count the "great" guitarists who made themselves famous with it, from Herb Ellis to Jim Hall and Joe Pass, and more recently Pat Metheny. Even a "pop" guitarist like Steve Howe shows a clear preference for the 175, despite his impressive guitar collection !

The ES-175 appeared for the first time in the Gibson catalog of August 1, 1949, which furthermore, to better illustrate the decline of the Hawaiian guitars to the advantage of the "Electric Spanish" type guitars, carried on its cover the brand new ES-5 that we will examine in more details later on.

The most remarkable characteristic of the ES-175 at the time of its introduction was a sharp Florentine cutaway instead of the rounded Venetian cutaway used until then. (With the exception perhaps of the style "0" Artist Model introduced in the early days).

Otherwise, the ES-175 could resemble an ES-125 by its dimensions — 161/4" × 20 1/4" × 3 3/8" — which besides a Florentine cutaway, would have received double parallelogram position markers of the L-7 or ES-350 type. It is to be noted, however, that because of its dimensions the 175 had a shorter fingerboard with a 24 3/4" scale length and 19 frets as opposed to 25 1/2" and 20 frets for the 350. The neck naturally joined the body at the fourteenth fret.

The body of the 175 was made entirely of laminated maple with a one piece mahogany neck and a bound rosewood fingerboard. The headstock had the "classic" crown inlay and the tailpiece was the "pointed" trapeze found on the ES-350 and ES-300.

As for the name "175", to understand it, one only needs to refer to the Gibson tradition, as the selling price of the instrument in August 1949 was ... $ 175.00 for the regular model (ES-175) and $ 190.00 for the "Natural" model (ES-175 N)...

At the time of its introduction in 1949, the ES-175 was only available with one single coil pick-up, situated near the fingerboard, though not close to it.

As typical of the early P 90 single coil units, the pick-up cover was narrower and made of a thicker material than on the subsequent models which have besides a much more square sided shape.

A double pick-up version designated **ES-175D** (or ES-175DN) was not offered to the public until 1953. According to the official shipping totals, the ES-175 was to enjoy a tremendous success as from the date of its introduction, although the single p.u. model saw a small decline in its popularity with the introduction of the 2 p.u. model.

On the other hand, the **ES-5** that Gibson also marketed starting in 1949 had a rather extraordinary feature for the time since it was equipped with 3 pick-ups !!!

The ES-5 was announced as the "supreme electronic version of the famed L-5", hence the name "ES (Electric Spanish) 5", and as such it was introduced as the most expensive item of the electric line.

The original ES-175 with
a 19 fret fingerboard and a
narrow pick-up cover.

Jim HALL

Joe PASS

Herb ELLIS

Gibson had determined that in order to obtain a greater variety of sounds, it was necessary to fill the space available between the fingerboard and the bridge !... it resulted in a three pick-up model.

The ES-5 was really a multiple sound guitar... each pick-up had a volume control and a careful dosing is all that was needed to achieve the required tonal coloring. A master tone control mounted on the upper cutaway bout completed the adjustements.

However this wiring had a major drawback as it did not enable the player to switch from one preset tone to another.

Otherwise the ES-5 used single coil pick-ups comparable to the ones found on the ES-300 or ES-350 and they do not require additional comments.

The ES-5 naturally had the same dimensions as the L-5 : 17" × 21" × 3 3/8", and like the ES-350, it was entirely made of curly maple, without the L-5's spruce carved top.

The fingerboard was made of rosewood — and not ebony — with rectangular pearl inlays, and in the fashion of the L-5, it was luxuriously trimmed and ended in a heart. However, the ES-5 did not exhibit the "Flower pot" inlay found on all the L-5's but the more ordinary Gibson "crown" inlay just like the ES-175. On the very first examples of ES-5 the "F" holes were not even bound.
The compensating bridge was entirely of rosewood, and vertically adjustable only at the extremities.

The ES-5 was, in all probability, the first stock electric guitar to be equipped with three pick-ups, despite many public claims in favour of a Californian competitor of Gibson a few years later... (guess who ?)

In August 1949, the ES-5 in Sunburst cost $ 375.00 while the "Blonde" ES-5N reached $ 390.00. It is nevertheless interesting to see that despite its price and its outrageous versatility which could not necessarily have been everybody's cup of tea, the ES-5 was manufactured in greater quantities than the ES-350 or ES-300.

In short, the Gibson electric catalog as at August 1, 1949 was offering the following models :

| | | |
|---|---|---|
| — ES-5 | : | $ 375.00 |
| — ES-5N | : | $ 390.00 |
| — ES-350 | : | $ 325.00 |
| — ES-350N | : | $ 340.00 |
| — ES-300 | : | $ 235.00 |
| — ES-300N | : | $ 250.00 |
| — L-7 CE* | : | $ 235.00 |
| — L-7 CED* | : | $ 265.00 |
| — ES-175 | : | $ 175.00 |
| — ES-175N | : | $ 190.00 |
| — ES-150 | : | $ 147.50 |
| — ES-125 | : | $ 97.50 |

* The models without a cutaway, L-7E and L-7ED, were actually available even though they were not mentioned in the catalog.

Gibson thus disposed of a well structured line of electric models with a 1 to 4 ratio in the price range. Just as for the pre-War acoustic models, Gibson was concerned in offering a complete electric line ranging from the "low-budget" to the "super-deluxe" model. The obvious goal was to make avalaible to the guitar enthusiast, regardless of his wealth, a good guitar worth the Gibson name.

# THE 1950's

After the avalanche of novelties that the budding electric guitar market had created just after the War, 1950 was somehow a quieter year, destined to consolidate the company's leadership. However, an additional building was erected on Parsons Street during this year to allow Gibson to satisfy the constant progression of its activities. It is interesting to note that this building still shelters today the offices of the Gibson management in Kalamazoo.

A new model, nevertheless, made its appearance in 1950, it was the **ES-140,** which would be better defined as a smaller size 175 ! As a matter of fact the Gibson literature of that time initially introduced the ES-140 as a "Three Quarter Size" ES-175.

Compared to the 175's 16 1/4" × 20 1/4" dimensions, the 140 had the relatively unsual size of 12 1/16" × 17 1/4" (original dimensions, later to be widened to 12 3/4"). The proportions however, were the same as well as the sharp Florentine cutaway.

The ES-140 was a guitar intended for young guitarists or for adults with small hands, as it provided a "short" neck with a 22 3/4" scale length compared to 24 3/4" for an ES-175 or 25 1/2" for an ES-350. The "scale

The regular ES-5 was introduced in 1949
with three single coil pick-ups.

A special order ES-5 N made in 1949 with only one pick-up.
Note the unbound "F" holes as typical of the early ES-5's.
This guitar has been fitted with an L-5 tailpiece and a Tune-O-Matic bridge.

This picture clearly shows the ES-140 was a small size ES-175. It only lacked double parallelogram position markers to make a perfect match. On this photo the 140 tailpiece is not original.

The CF-100 E introduced in 1951.

ES 140. The first "Three quarter size" electric introduced by Gibson in 1950.

In the early fifties the ES-350 received what is now considered as the standard Gibson wiring with dual volume and tone controls and a 3-position toggle switch. On this instrument the tailpiece is not original.

length", refers to the distance between the bridge and the nut, and it quite logically influences the dimensions of the fret-spaces. The smaller the space, the "easier" the playing of the guitar for the beginner. The model supplied with this "short" type neck took the designation "3/4" or Three Quarter Size.

The fingerboard of the 140 still had 19 frets and its neck joined the body at the fourteenth fret. Except for a shorter trapeze shaped tail-piece and smaller "F" holes, the 140 had a single coil pick-up with volume and tone controls identical to the ones on the 175.

The ES-140 was offered starting in 1950 with only a sunburst finish and sold for the easily understandable price of $ 140.00 ! It was only in its last year of existence before being definitely replaced in 1956 by the 140T model that a small number of 140's with a "Natural" finish were released by the factory.

Often, like the other "Three Quarter Size" models, the ES-140 can appear like a "toy", but it is an utterly professional instrument, carefully built and with a surprising sound and playing quality. This does explain why hundreds of ES-140 were sold as soon as the model was introduced.

In the meantime some purely aesthetic modifications were to take place on the two biggest selling Gibson models of the early fifties namely : the ES-125 and the ES-150.

As a matter of fact, right after the War, the ES-125 was sporting "plastic" trapazoidal position markers while the "more expensive" ES-150, had only pearl dot position markers.

Around 1949, the ES-125 lost its "crowns" in favour of dots.

Then, around 1951, the ES-150, in turn, was given trapazoidal position markers... as if to re-establish some hierarchy in the line. Beyond the anecdote, this evolution in the specifications can help to determine the age, or at least the period when such a model was manufactured.

To tell the difference between a 125 and a post-War 150, one of the simplest things to remember is that : the ES-150 with its body size of 17" × 21" is 3/4" longer and wider than the 125.

In the early fifties, the ES-125 was also equipped with a regular P90 pick-up with adjustable pole pieces identical to the one on the 150.

Then in 1951, a rather unusual model was introduced to complete the Gibson line of electric guitars, it was the **CF-100E,** who offered some unusual features because :

a) it was a small "Flat Top" guitar, with a round sound hole ;

b) it had a Florentine cutaway ;

c) it was supplied with a pick-up mounted at the end of the fingerboard.

These characteristics had never been brought together before on one guitar.

The CF-100E with its relatively modest dimensions — 14 1/8" × 19 1/2" × 4 3/8" originally later certain catalogs will indicate 14 1/4" × 19" — had a spruce top and mahogany back and rims. Its fingerboard and bridge were rosewood. The neck had 19 frets for a normal scale length of 24 3/4" and was enhanced by trapezoidal position markers. The Gibson "crown" design was inlaid on the peg head.

The CF-100E was equipped with a narrow single coil pick-up (with adjustable pole pieces) located at the end of the fingerboard. The only available finish was the traditional "Chocolate Brown" with a golden sunburst on top.

A purely acoustic version appeared simultaneously under the name CF 100.

However after its reasonably successful introduction on the market in 1951, the CF-100E peaked in 1952 and its production started to decline slowly afterwards until its withdrawal a few years later.

Besides the CF-100E, two other novelties were to appear in 1951 and complete the line in a much more lasting and significant manner. Indeed at the Gotham Hotel in New-York, Ted MacCarty and Julius Bellson unveiled in 1951 the all new Super 400 CES and L-5 CES.

With them, Gibson had just taken the "last step" in amplification, by offering an electrified version of its two most prestigeous acoustic guitars, which thus were to become the two top-of-the-lines in the electric range.

## THE L-5 CES AND SUPER 400 CES

The "L-5" had been created originally by Lloyd Loar in 1923 in the "Master Model" series and then modified in 1935 with an enlarged body of 17" wide (Advanced Model) compared to the 16 1/4" of Loar's model. Around 1936 it was given a fancy gold/silver tailpiece marked L-5, then beginning in 1939, a version with a Venitian cutaway became available under the name L-5 "Premier". It is also at this time that the first natural finish editions appeared.

The "L-5P" became the "L-5C" around 1949, and this was the model Gibson chose to electrify making it the **L-5CES** (Cutaway Electric Spanish).

Unlike the post-War ES type electric models, the L-5CES as well as the Super 400 CES did have a solid carved top made of spruce, and not of laminated maple. "Electrically" speaking, a solid top was not of so much importance, but Gibson could not bring out two distinct types of L-5 or Super 400, one acoustic with a solid top, the other electric with a laminated top.

The solid back and rims were of maple, with wonderful curls or bird's eyes, while the neck was of laminated curly maple with an ebony fingerboard. Rectangular pearl blocks and multiple bindings were inlaid in the ebony fingerboard characterized by its pointed ending.

Lastly, the most particular characteristic of the "L-5" from an aesthetic point of view is undoubtedly its "Flower pot" (or torch) inlay on the peg-head. This beautiful ornament was first originated on the Gibson mandolins around 1911 and it was a regular feature on the F-4, albeit in a longer version, because of the lack of truss rod cover until the early twenties.

The "Super 400" for its part had been conceived in 1934 with a "Super Grand Auditorium" body of more than 18" wide ! Around the end of the 1930's the design was slightly changed and the upper bout somewhat enlarged. Like the "L-5", the Super 400 became available with a cutaway and natural finish starting in late 1939.

The "Super 400" naturally had a solid spruce top, with solid back and rims of flamed maple as well as a laminated curly maple neck with an ebony fingerboard. However, compared with the L-5, the Super 400 was charcaterized besides the body dimensions, by a longer peg-head decorated with a "split" diamond, which later on became the symbol of the "Custom" models. Also to be noted were the more sophisticated "split block" pearl position markers, along with the typically elongated "F" holes.

Until around 1955, the Super 400 was given a narrow purfling inside its Venitian cutaway. Then, a wider purfing was used in order to adapt to the height of the arch top. Moreover the shape of the round cutaway changed over the years and it tends to be less "open" on recent models as opposed to the fifties.

As for the pick-ups, the L-5 CES and the Super 400 CES were originally equipped with two single coil pick-ups like the ones commonly used by Gibson at this time.

Then, around 1952, the Gibson engineers Walt Fuller and Seth Lover perfected a new pick-up currently nicknamed "Alnico" pick-up because it has six oblong Alnico V magnets placed directly under the strings... Gibson's objective with this new pick-up whose magnets were adjustable in height was to obtain a better sensitivity, and thus, a more balanced, but also a more powerful sound than with the regular single coil pick-up. The magnets of this new pick-up were stronger, being real Alnico V instead of the weaker Alnico II or IV. On the other hand, this single coil still had 10,000 turns of number 42 wire, the most commonly used wire for high impedance guitar pick-ups.

This sophisticated conception naturally destined the "Alnico" pick-up for the most "luxurious" models of the electric line, such as the Super 400 CES, the L-5 CES and later on the Les Paul Custom or the Byrdland. However, a certain number of ES-175 models were also fitted with this unit, either on a special order basis or to accomodate the existing stock or simply to promote the latest Gibson pick-up.

Against all expectations it seems though that the more delicate tuning of the "Alnico" pick-up, compared to regular P-90 pick-up, might have hurt its scope, as it proved to be less "popular" than perhaps Gibson had thought it would be.

This is likely to be the reason why a great number of L-5 CES and even a few Super 400 guitars are found today with P-90 single coil pick-up and not the "Alnico" type. It is diffi-

L-5 CES (1955)
with Alnico pick-ups.

The L-5 headstock with its graceful flower pot inlay.

Kenny BURRELL
with a SUPER 400.

### THE SUPER-400 CES
### ELECTRIC SPANISH CUTAWAY GUITAR

One of the finest electric Spanish guitars ever developed, the Super-400 CES has been given enthusiastic approval by the nation's outstanding musicians.

A definite factor in the quality of tone and responsiveness of the Super-400 CES is the carved spruce top, an unusual feature in an electric guitar. The finest spruce, curly maple and rosewood add to the beauty of this instrument, available in Natural (as shown), or the Gibson Golden Sunburst finish.

- The two pick-ups are set close to the bridge and fingerboard for wider contrast in tone color.
- Modern cutaway design and small neck for fast, easy action.
- Gibson Tune-O-Matic bridge and extra large, individually adjustable Alnico No. 5 magnets give greater sustaining power and perfect accuracy from each string.
- Pick-ups have adjustable pole pieces and separate tone and volume controls which can be pre-set.
- Three-position toggle switch on treble side activates either or both pick-ups.
- Decorative accents to the beauty of the Super-400 CES include gold plated metal parts, pearl inlays and ivoroid binding.

*Super-400 CES Electric Spanish Cutaway Guitar—Golden Sunburst Finish.*
*Super-400 CESN Electric Spanish Cutaway Guitar—Natural Finish.*
*Cases for above instruments—*
*400 Faultless*

Scotty MOORE with the Blonde L-5 CES he used when playing with Elvis Presley.

Excerpt from the 1954 catalog depicting the SUPER 400 CES.

cult to give an accurate estimate of the proportion but it was practically half-and-half for the L-5 CES. On some guitars the equipment was "mixed" with an Alnico pick-up and a P-90 pick-up. Some L-5 CES's were also equipped at the factory with only one pick-up instead of two.

From their introduction, the Super 400 CES and the L-5 CES were given separate volume and tone controls for each pick-up, with a three-position toggle switch.

Both models were introduced simultaneously but it seems that the electric version of the L-5 was "created" and put into production slightly before the Super 400, as suggested by the shipping totals we were able to obtain from Gibson. As a matter of fact, the Super 400 CES was not shipped in quantity until 1952, while the L-5 CES had already been launched starting in 1951.

The available finishes were, of course, the traditional "sunburst" and for a small extra charge, a "natural" finish, which set off the quality of the carefully selected wood for both models.

Through the years the Super 400 CES was to make itself famous in the hands of guitarists such as Kenny Burrell, Merle Travis, Larry Coryell, Louis Stewart or Eric Gale. The "L-5 CES", for its part, was adopted by the great Wes Montgomery and, for some time by, George Benson, not to forget Elvis Presley's first guitarist, Scotty Moore, who used an "L-5" before switching over to a "Super 400" to lay down the basics of rock guitar !

The introduction of these two models in 1951 can be regarded as a sort of high point for the "amplified" acoustic guitar, for in 1952 a new type of purely electric guitar was to make its appearance and progressively revolutionize the market. We are speaking, of course, of the Les Paul series guitar, to which the entire next chapter is devoted.

# CHAPTER 3

# THE FIRST "SOLID BODY" GUITARS THE ORIGINAL LES PAUL SERIES 1952-1961

The introduction of a "Solid Body" guitar by Gibson in 1952 can appear as a logical extension of the company's efforts to "electrify" a guitar, if we take into account the great popularity of the "Hawaiian" guitars. These guitars were actually the first "solid body" guitars, as the body and neck could be made either of wood or metal (mainly aluminium) depending on the model. Consequently the idea of an instrument with no "acoustic quality" using only a pick-up to be heard was not new. All the same, if we disregard the musical context in which they were most often used, Hawaiian guitars have a very particular sound, which is perhaps at the origin of the non-Hawaiian "solid body" guitar. As the making of this type of instrument did not pose any particularly difficult technical problem or require a superior craftmanship, one could say without the shadow of a doubt, that it was easy for Gibson to manufacture a "solid body" before 1952.

The "father" of such an instrument is, furthermore, difficult to distinguish for sure but Rickenbacker, under the circumstances, seems to be in the best position, first of all for its "frying pan" introduced in 1931, but especially thanks to its "Electro" Spanish Guitar series of 1935. This guitar is, to our knowledge, the first non-Hawaiian "Solid Body" guitar ever commercialized (with Vivitone).

Be that as it may — and as paradoxical as that can seem — the man who was going to lead Gibson into the solid body venture is named... Clarence Leo Fender !

Leo Fender was certainly not the first — even though some may say so — to conceive or even to put into regular production a "solid body" guitar. Moreover, if care is taken to look at certain guitars of the same period — like those made by Paul Bigsby in the forties — one can even doubt the sheer originality of the first Fender guitars. On the other hand, there is one undisputable fact, Leo Fender was the first to achieve commercial success with a solid body guitar.

Fender introduced the "Broadcaster" model in 1948 under the rather amused eye of the different "great" names of the guitar business of the time who were full of reservations about the idea of manufacturing "planks". The Fender attempt was nevertheless followed with interest — one never knows ! — each one telling himself that in essence you did not have to be very qualified to produce this type of guitar, which really lacked finesse of craftmanship. However a number of guitarists, especially in the "Country Music" field found great advantages in these "planks of wood", either because of their clear sound, their easy handling, or their playing comfort.

By 1950 Gibson was convinced that the "solid body" guitar was here to stay and consequently, it had to offer a model. Now, as Ted MacCarty, who became president of Gibson in 1950, tells it with a big smile "we needed an excuse !... and that excuse was going to be Mr Les Paul !..."

## LESTER W. POLFUS

With the real name of Lester William Polfus, Les Paul was born on June 9, 1916 in Waukesha, Wisconsin. He initially intended to be a pianist, and the guitar was only his second love ; however, an Art Tatum recording allegedly convinced him to dedicate himself instead to the guitar, which was then in the early stages of its "modern era".

At the beginning of the 1930's, Lester Polfus moved to Chicago where, under the "Les Paul" name, he played jazz on the station WIND, and Country music on WJJD as "Rhubarb Red" (he eventually dropped this name in 1936).

While gaining some reputation as a guitarist, Les Paul started experimenting with the idea of amplifying his guitar, by adding, for example, a phonograph pick-up.

Then he began to cut and "customize" an increasing number of guitars to achieve the "sound" he wanted. In this sort of trial and error process Les Paul, himself, confessed to having massacred a great deal of instruments in order to perfect the placing of a pick-up or to overcome the problems of feed back. Starting in 1934, he had succeeded in creating a sufficiently powerful and efficient pick-up that could be used on the radio or in public !

In 1937, Les Paul decided to try his luck in New-York with his trio of the time which included Jimmy Atkins, Chet's brother. Thanks to boldness and talent, he succeeded in obtaining recognition in the artistic spheres of the town.

Around the end of the 1930's, he became very interested in recording and particularly in the problems of "Re-Recording" or recording "sound on sound". In this field which was then in its infant stage, Les Paul was to play a role of pioneer and innovator which, in collaboration with Ampex, lead to the appearance of the first eight track tape recorder in 1952.

Back to the guitar, he asked Epiphone in 1941 to allow him to use their plant on Sunday, in order to pursue his experiments. It is at Epi that "the Log" — a 4" × 4" piece of wood prepared like a guitar with a Gibson neck — was born.

In 1943, Les Paul decided to leave for Los Angeles to accompany Bing Crosby, before devoting himself to a solo career with vocalist Mary Ford (born Coleen Summers).

Just after the War, Les Paul asked Gibson to produce a guitar according to his specifications but he was politely rejected by Maurice Berlin who refused the proposition and even called his guitar a "broom stick" ! Gibson's image was at the time too well established to run the risk of being hurt by an attempt, original to be sure, but too hazardous.

Beginning in 1949, Les Paul did, however, meet with success since his recording with Mary Ford were nicely climbing the "charts" to the top. "Lover", "How High the Moon", "Brazil"... became number one and made Les Paul one of the most popular artists of the early 1950's.

Its is because of his status as a star, his reputation as a guitarist and as a sound "wizard", that Gibson was keen to make contact with Les Paul and asked him to lend his name to the solid body guitar the company planned to introduce.

# THE CONCEPTION OF THE PROTOTYPE

The prototype of what was to become "**The Les Paul Guitar**" was conceived by the Gibson R & D department around 1950/1951. The idea of a "solid body" guitar was in itself simple, yet it was necessary to define what materials this "plank of wood" would be made of. The problem was solved through successive experiments with different types of wood, and also with other types of materials. It has been said that a prototype was even made using piece of rail from a railroad track !

Since the woods commonly used in the guitar industry at that time were not that numerous, Gibson finally opted for a combination of mahogany and maple. As a matter of fact, mahogany was acceptable mainly because of its weight but it lacked somehow the ability to hold the sound or "sustain", whereas maple — much denser than mahogany — gave a satisfying sustain but was too heavy. A combination of both woods — mahogany with maple on top — offered an ideal compromise between the weight and the sustain the new model needed. It is interesting to note the two woods glued together were in fact cut differently as mahogany was used with a vertical grain while maple had an horizontal grain.

Ted MacCarty and his team were obliged to somewhat reduce the dimensions of the proto-

LES PAUL and MARY FORD in the early fifties.
The original picture dedicated by the artists is hung
on the walls of the Gibson management offices in Kalamazoo.
We are thankful to Jim Deurloo for supplying us with this document.

type in comparison to a regular electric acoustic model, in order to give it a total weight acceptable to the majority of guitarists.

It would have been unrealistic to make a solid body guitar with a 16 1/4" or 17" width, even if it were very thin. The prototype, therefore, kept a guitar shape that could be termed as rather "traditional" but, with a width of only 12 3/4", a length of 17 1/4" and a depth of 1 3/4" at the rim.

Lastly it was Gibson's idea to give the new guitar a "carved" maple top since it had two distinct and interesting advantages :

1° it allowed the future "solid body" guitar to better assimilate with a regular guitar;

2° it necessitated a tooling that competitors such as Fender did not possess at the time.

Thus the new Gibson model would be really different and also... more difficult to copy. By the way the carved top of the original Les Paul guitars is noticeably different — i.e somewhat higher and flatter with also flatter surroundings — from the one on the more recent models of the series, undoubtedly due to a change in the tooling equipment... but this modification naturally has no influence on the actual sound of the guitar.

The prototype was given a one-piece mahogany Gibson neck with a rosewood fingerboard, but is must be pointed out that this neck had 22 frets, instead of 19 or 20, and that the junction with the body was at the sixteenth fret and not at the fourteenth like the electric acoustic guitars of that period. Access to the upper registers was facilitated by the adoption of a new style Venetian cutaway, slightly less rounded.

Two single coil P 90 type pick-ups were mounted with independent volume and tone controls for each unit plus a three-position toggle switch so that each pick-up could be used separately or both simultaneously.

Lastly, two interesting points concerning this Gibson prototype are worth noticing. It was initially equipped with a traditional trapeze tailpiece similar to the ones on the electric acoustic guitars of the period, and not with the long trapeze tailpiece eventually featured on the first issue.

Then, as regards the gold top finish, opinions are somewhat divided as Les Paul himself claimed he insisted on the gold color so that the guitar looked "more expensive". However, according to Ted MacCarty the prototype was already painted gold when it was shown to Les Paul. In any case, besides any aesthetic consideration, the gold top finish enabled Gibson to conceal the upper maple piece. Thus no one could realize that the guitar was of mahogany and maple... the prototype could appear to be carved from a single piece of mahogany.

As a support to this theory the 1952 catalog, in which the "Les Paul" model was presented for the first time mentioned a mahogany body but said nothing about maple. However, considering the thinness of the plastic bindings used at this time on the original Les Paul series, it was possible for anyone to catch a glimpse of maple inside the cutaway and see that the upper part was of a much clearer wood than the body.

After finishing the prototype, Gibson briefly wondered how to reconcile its reputation with the need to launch the new model on a market which was in full evolution. It needed a reason, a sort of excuse... so Gibson thought of Les Paul. He was an excellent guitarist and a very popular artist and, lastly, he apparenly, persisted then in not wanting to play on a Gibson guitar ! Considering that the new instrument might more than interest Les Paul, Ted MacCarty made an appointment with him through his financial adviser, Phil Braunstein. The meeting took place in Pennsylvania at Delaware Water Gap, where Les Paul was recording with Mary Ford.

After briefly playing on the prototype Les Paul, according to Ted MacCarty, said the following words to Mary Ford : "I think we should join them, now because they are really getting too close !"

Ted MacCarty suggested that Les Paul should "lend" his name to the new guitar in exchange for a royalty on each model sold. In fact, the contract between Les Paul and Gibson was drawn up the very night of the presentation, by Phil Braunstein, Les Paul and Ted MacCarty. Under the terms of this contract established on a renewable five-year basis, Les Paul was no longer to appear in public without playing on a Gibson, and the royalties were not payable until the end of every five years for this reason and also for tax purposes.

Ted MacCarty asked Les Paul if he had

The LES PAUL model introduced in 1952

LES PAUL model (1954)

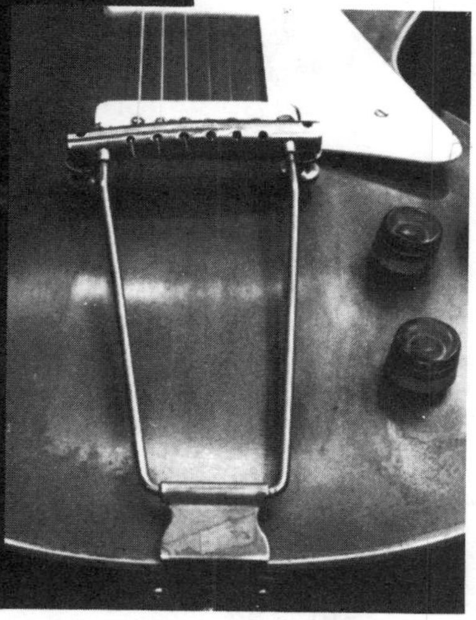

The combination trapeze bridge-tailpiece perfected by Les Paul for the original Les Paul model. Note the strings are pulled "under" the bar.

## THE GIBSON LES PAUL GUITAR

*Les Paul and Mary Ford*

The famed "Les Paul tones" can now become a reality for all guitar players with this beautiful, solid body Les Paul guitar, incorporating many unusual Gibson features. Striking in appearance with its gold-finished, carved maple top, mahogany body and neck, the Les Paul name is in gold script on the peghead of this model.

A unique, new feature is the metal combination bridge and tailpiece, with the strings making contact on top of the bridge and adjustable both horizontally and vertically. This new style bridge and tailpiece enables the player to dampen the tone with the heel of the picking hand for muffled "Les Paul tones."

- Two pickups have separate tone and volume controls.
- Three position toggle switch activates either or both pickups.
- Tone can be pre-set to any desired quality and change from one pickup to another can be accomplished by a flip of the toggle switch.
- No dead notes—clear, sustaining tones in all positions with the 22 fret fingerboard.
- No buildup of synthetic tones or feed back.
- Body size—length, 17 ¼", width 12 ¾"; scale length, 24 ¾".

*Les Paul Solid Body Electric Spanish Cutaway Guitar*

*Case for Les Paul Model*

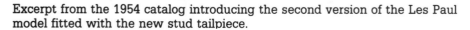

Excerpt from the 1954 catalog introducing the second version of the Les Paul model fitted with the new stud tailpiece.

The Les Paul headstock with the Gibson logo inlaid in pearl and the words "Les Paul model" silk-screened in yellow letters.

any suggestions concerning the prototype, and Les proposed the new combination bridge-tailpiece he had just perfected. This combination bridge-tailpiece was characterized by a cylindrical bar placed at the end of a traditional tailpiece, and around which the strings were wrapped. The Gibson tailpiece was, therefore, replaced by the unit designed by Les Paul, which, moreover, gave the guitar a slightly different sonority.

Les Paul, of course, gave Gibson the sole rights to this new tailpiece, which was offered among the company's other accessories.

The contract between Gibson and Les Paul was signed and the first "Les Paul" guitars were soon introduced in the spring of 1952.

Meanwhile, Gibson had overcome its reservations and had gone back on its original decision not to put its name on the guitar... The new "Les Paul" was therefore introduced as a Gibson !

The peg-head was given the brands's logo inlaid in pearl, with the words "Les Paul Model" in yellow letters perpendicular to "Gibson". Lastly, the guitar was fitted with six Kluson tuning machines (at this time the name of the manufacturer did not appear on the cover of the tuners) with plastic "tulip" buttons.

For a historical sidelight, guitar enthusiasts will no doubt have noted that in spite of his many talents, Les Paul had apparently little to do with the creation of the model carrying his name. According to Ted MacCarty the first Les Paul guitar was entirely designed by the Gibson R & D dept in a cooperative effort, with the exception of the tailpiece which was suggested by Les Paul. However, Les Paul himself said on a number of occasions that he was definitely involved in the basic conception of the instrument, owing to his long experience in the field of solid body guitars. It is difficult to assess exactly "who did what", some thirty years after the event took place, since accurate recollections are likely to dim as time goes by. In any case, Les Paul was to become a valuable consultant for Gibson from the time of the agreement and his opinion was always carefully considered ever-since.

At the same time as the guitar, Gibson also introduced a 12-watt Les Paul amplifier which carried the initials L.P. on the front grill.

The "Les Paul" legend had just begun...

# THE FIRST LES PAUL MODEL

The beginnings of the new "Les Paul" model were rather satisfying if the Gibson shipping totals are used as a reference, since the figures reached in 1952 or 1953 are considerably higher than those of the electric range except for the 125 model. Gibson had not missed its entry into the "barbarian" world of the solid body guitar !

Throughout the 1950's, Gibson was going to create a whole range of guitars based on this first Les Paul introduced in 1952. Besides, the original model itself was to undergo a certain number of modifications, as no less than five variants of the "Les Paul" model, then Standard, appeared between 1952 and 1960.

The first issue — in other words the original model — was characterized by :

- two single coil magnetic pick-ups with white plastic covers (which are affectionately known as "soap bars"). On the first white plastic cover P 90, the material is slightly thinner than on later pick-ups ;
- a Les Paul type trapeze bridge-tailpiece with the strings pulled under the bridge ;
- a gold finish on the top with the rest of the body and the neck of mahogany. The shade of the mahogany body can be darker or lighter depending on the guitar.

This variant, as well as the three following ones, are usually called "**Gold Top**" to distinguish them from the well known "Sunburst" model which was the fifth and last original variant.

Some Les Paul models were offered in a "Solid Gold" version with the body and the neck entirely finished in gold paint. These all gold models are much rarer than the "Gold Tops".

The Les Paul models manufactured in 1952 and at the beginning of 1953 do not carry a serial number as Gibson did not set up a numbering system for solid body guitars until 1953 (see appendix III).

The very first Les Paul guitars can be identified by the absence of binding on the fingerboard, as well as the diagonal position of the two screws on the pick-up near the bridge, and the height of the gold tinted plastic knobs (nicknamed "hat box knobs" or "speed knobs").

Very quickly, the trapeze bridge-tailpiece posed problems in not enabling guitarists to muffle the strings with the picking hand. Besides for those used to playing with the hand resting on the bridge, the strings were much too low and the playing comfort was hindered.

Thus around the end of 1953, the Les Paul model was modified so that it could receive the new bridge-tailpiece perfected by the Gibson R & D department as early as 1952. This new tailpiece, frequently called "stop" tailpiece or "stud" tailpiece necessitated an enlargement of the neck angle with the body. Therefore, more than any other detail, the positioning of the neck allows the first Les Paul guitars of the 1952-1953 period to be easily identified, even if the Les Paul bridge-tailpiece has been taken off, and replaced.

This second variant otherwise identical to the first one was officially introduced in early 1954, but a certain number of Les Paul guitars with 1953 serial numbers were fitted with a stop tailpiece, demonstrating that the change rather took place at the end of 1953.

As regards its finish, the second variant was similar to the first one, including, the fact that-some were painted all-gold. In fact, this option stayed available as long as "Gold Top" guitars were produced, but it was used much more for the first two variants equipped with the Les Paul trapeze bridge-tailpiece or with the stop tailpiece than for the following models with the Tune-O-Matic bridge.

# LES PAUL CUSTOM, JUNIOR, SPECIAL

As early as 1954, Gibson consolidated its line of solid body guitars by matching the "Les Paul Model" with a "deluxe" and an "economy" versions.

## THE LES PAUL CUSTOM

The "deluxe" model — (designated the **Les Paul Custom)** — was given an ebony fingerboard with rectangular pearl block position markers, while the body had multiple bindings on the upper as well as one on the lower edges. Naturally all the metal parts were gold plated.

The Les Paul Custom, in contrast to the regular model from which it came, was made entirely of mahogany without a maple top.

This all mahogany body can be explained three ways. The **appearance...,** as a matter of fact, Ted MacCarty points out that since the guitar was lacquered black, it was not necessary to give the new model a maple top. The **cost...** a guitar made entirely of mahogany naturally cost less. The **sonority...** because mahogany produced a sound a little "mellower" than maple, and Gibson was introducing the Custom mainly as a jazz guitar.

The first explanation is questionable, for it is hard to see why Gibson would have insisted on having maple under gold paint and not under black paint, when in each case, the wood is not visible.

Consequently, only the second and third explanations seem worth taking into account.

At this stage it must be said that the maple used on the Les Paul "Gold Top" guitars (or should we say "under" the Gold Top !) was, most of the time, of excellent quality and finely curled, albeit in two, three, or even four pieces not necessarily book-matched. Consequently, it is difficult to imagine Gibson looking to save money on its Custom model !

Aside from an entirely mahogany body, the other peculiarity of the "Les Paul Custom" lied in its pick-ups, as two different types were used. In the "rhythm" position, Gibson put an "Alnico" pick-up with six oblong Alnico V type magnets, while in the "lead" position the Custom had a P 90 type single coil pick-up, identical to those on the Les Paul model.

The goal was to give the instrument greater tone possibilities by varying the parameters (thus perhaps the reason for the entirely mahogany body ?)

The Les Paul Custom, which naturally had the same dimensions as the standard model, was first offered in 1954, exclusively in the "Ebony" finish (opaque black), which very quickly earned it the nickname "Black Beauty". The model was also frequently called the "Fretless Wonder" because of its smooth extra-flat frets.

The headstock featuring the split diamond inlay originated on the SUPER 400.

LES PAUL CUSTOM (1954)
The gold tinted knobs
are not original

The Alnico pick-up used in the rhythm position. Note the two screws in diagonal holding the unit onto the body.

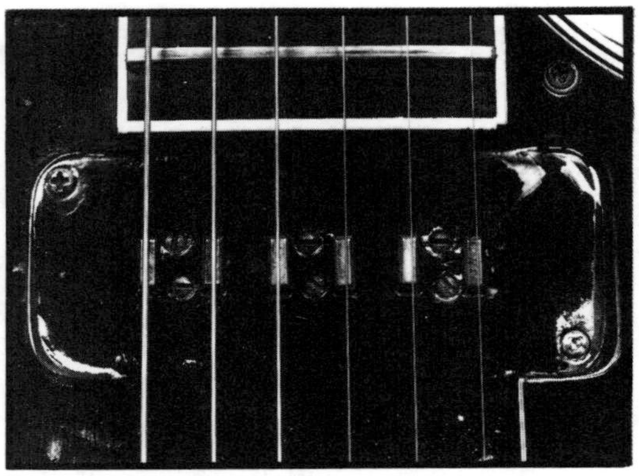

The black finish used on the original Custom models is different from the finish on the guitars reintroduced starting in 1968. The original finish, in fact, looks "blacker" but not as "deep", as it has fewer coats of clear varnish over the black paint.

At the time of its introduction in 1954, the Les Paul Custom was equipped with a "Tune-O-Matic" type bridge — that is, adjustable string by string for intonation thanks to small moving saddles — and not the combination bridge-stop-tailpiece that was used up to the end of 1955 on the standard model.

The "Tune-O-Matic" bridge was perfected by Ted MacCarty and his team as early as 1952 so as to be able to be adapted to any kind of guitar with or without an arched top. The goal was to obtain a bridge that could take into account the different length adjustments of a string to perfect the pitch. Besides the Custom, the "Tune-O-Matic" bridge, was quickly adapted to several of the brand's top models.

The Les Paul Custom was, lastly, given a peg-head a little wider than the Les Paul model, on which the Super 400's "split" diamond was inlaid. The gold plated Kluson tuning machines were initially identical to the ones on the "Les Paul Model", then, later on, Kluson life-time lubricated "Sealfast" tuning machines were fitted. As for the words "Les Paul Custom", they were embossed on the truss rod cover.

From its introduction, the "Black Beauty" was adopted by, among others, Frank Beecher, lead guitarist with Bill Haley, the creator of the famous "Rock around the Clock", but it also proved popular among some jazz or rhythm and blues players.

## LES PAUL JUNIOR

The "economy" model introduced as the **Les Paul Junior** also appeared in 1954, and was slightly more remote from the model it was based upon as it did not have a carved upper part.

In fact, the Junior was really a 12 3/4" × 17 1/4" × 1 3/4" "slab" of mahogany taking on only the form of a Les Paul guitar. Moreover it had only one single coil type pick-up whose black plastic cover was characterized by two "ears" on each side to allow for the surface mounting of the unit. Only two controls for volume and tone, completed this basic electric equipment.

The neck was of a single piece of mahogany with an unbound rosewood fingerboard fitted with pearl dot position markers.

However its is worth noticing that the Junior's neck was slightly wider than the other two Les Paul guitars with 43 mm at the nut and nearly 53 mm at the 12th fret, and it was to remain so until the discontinuation of the original Les Paul series.

The Junior model was equipped with the same combination bridge-tailpiece used on the standard model of the time. As opposed to the two other Les Paul guitars, the Gibson logo was not inlaid in pearl, but simply silkscreemed in gold letters. The words "Les Paul Junior" were written in yellow letters perpendicular to the Gibson name. The Kluson tuning machines were in two rows of three keys each following the most economical formula.

The Junior was offered in a dark mahogany finish on the body and the neck, with a brown-into-yellow sunburst on top and a black plastic scratch-plate. However, from 1954 on, some Juniors were equally made with a yellow ivory finish, which starting in 1957. officially took on the "**TV**" designation, allegedly because it showed better on monochrome TV.

Introduced by mid-1954, the Les Paul Junior was quickly manufactured (and sold !) in huge quantities far exceeding those of the Custom and the regular models owing to its excellent value for money.

Thanks to its heavily distorted sound when played at high volumes, the Junior was later adopted by numerous hard-rock guitar players, such as Leslie West, in the early seventies.

In the Gibson price list of September 1, 1954 the Les Paul line was reading as follows :

| | |
|---|---|
| — Les Paul Deluxe : | $ 325.00 |
| — Les Paul Model : | $ 225.00 |
| — Les Paul Junior : | $ 99.50 |

It is of interest to note that in this list the "**Custom**" was in fact called "**Deluxe**", however the term "Custom" quickly replaced "Deluxe" in accordance with the wording on the truss rod cover.

*"65" LES PAUL Model (1953).*
*This particular instrument bearing serial number 3-1941 was certainly among the very first Gold-Tops fitted with a stud tailpiece. The white P-90's are deeply sunk into the body as on the Gold-Tops with a trapeze-bridge tailpiece.*

*"66" LES PAUL Custom (1956)... otherwise known as the "Black Beauty". The original Custom was also nicknamed the "Fretless Wonder" because of its smooth extra flat frets.*
*Note the Alnico pick-up in the rhythm position.*

*"67" Steve HACKETT, formerly with Genesis, playing a 1958 LES PAUL Gold-Top with Humbuckers.*

*"68" Jimmy PAGE with his 1959 LES PAUL Standard.*

*"69" A very nice pair of LES PAUL Standards. These two guitars clearly evidence the variations in the tiger striping of the flame maple top, as well as the way the sunburst finish can actually fade out with time. The 1958 example on the left has turned orange, while the 1960 model on the right has kept more red pigment from the original "Cherry Sunburst" finish.*
*The bank notes in the fore front give just a faint idea of what these guitars are worth some twenty years after their introduction.*

*"70" — **Top left :** Eric CLAPTON with the 1958 EXPLORER he used in the mid-seventies when he resumed touring.*
*— A perfect display of Modernistic Guitars... this particular Flying V has an original black fingerrest and jack plate with gold-plated metal parts. The Explorer always had a white scratch plate with nickel-plated parts.*

*"71" A truely mint 1958 "Flying V" in its original brown hard case with pink plush lining.*

*"72" — **Top left :** LES PAUL Special (1957) with limed mahogany finish. On this instrument, the original stud tailpiece has been replaced by a "Badass" type bridge.*
***— Top right :** A double cutaway LES PAUL Junior from 1960.*
***— Center :** SGC Special (1960).*
*This model was first introduced in 1959 as a LES PAUL Special — with LES PAUL markings on the headstock — but it was soon redesignated "SG Special" (SG : solid guitar) without any change in the specifications.*

Gibson

Gibson

Gibson

Gibson

Gibson

Gibson

## LES PAUL SPECIAL

After such "deluxe" and "economy" versions, Gibson soon starded working on an "intermediate" guitar destined to fill in the gap between the regular model and the truly low budget Les Paul Junior. This intermediate model took the designation **Les Paul Special** and was introduced in 1955 .

The "Special" was, for all purpose, a "Junior" equipped with two single coil pick-ups instead of one, with distinct volume and tone controls for each pick-up, plus a 3-position toggle switch. The pick-ups were mounted with the same rectangular covers used on the Les Paul model — albeit in black instead of white plastic — and lacked the dog's ears found on the Junior's pick-up.

Like the Junior, the Les Paul Special was flat and only retained the shape of the original Les Paul model without a carved top on its mahogany body. The bound fingerboard was made of rosewood with pearl dot position markers and the Gibson logo was inlaid in pearl on the peg-head, with the words "Les Paul Special" written in the usual yellow letters.

The finish was actually very "special" as it was a sort of straw-yellow (but not opaque) known as " limed mahogany". This finish very quickly became assimilated with the "TV" finish already in use on some Juniors even though no catalog ever officially used such a designation for a "Les Paul Special".

The original single cutaway Special was always associated with this "limed" finish and if some rare specials were **originally** delivered in Sunburst like a Junior it was only on a custom order basis. Lastly it was always offered — like the Junior — with a stud tailpiece and never fitted with a Tune-O-Matic bridge.

The Les Paul Special was listed on September 15, 1955 at the price of $ 169.50 whilst the Custom retailed at $ 360, the Standard at $ 235 and the Junior at $ 110.

In the latter part of 1955 the original Les Paul model — often called "Standard" although this name was not officially used by Gibson until 1958 — was modified for the third time since its introduction. This third variant is characterized by the adoption of the Tune-O-Matic bridge already used on the Les Paul Custom. Outside this modification, the "Les Paul Model" remained indentical to the preceding versions from a specification viewpoint.

In 1956, the only novelty consisted in the appearance of a "3/4" version of the Les Paul Junior with a scale length of 22 3/4" instead of 24 3/4". The fingerboard of the "3/4" version had 19 frets instead of 22 and the neck joined the body at the fourteenth fret instead of the sixteenth. Except for its "short" neck, the Les Paul Junior "3/4" was otherwise strictly identical to the regular edition and cost the same price.

# THE APPEARANCE OF THE HUMBUCKING PICK-UP

1957 was an especially important year for Gibson as it marked the official introduction of the "**Humbucking**" pick-up.

Let us see more in details how Gibson arrived at the conception of this type of pick-up which, nearly twenty five years after its introduction, is still the main electronic equipment of today's Gibson guitars. After different variations on the principle of the single coil pick-up, which culminated in the "Alnico" unit with 6 adjustable magnets, Gibson decided as early as 1953 to work on a new type of pick-up which, while keeping the tone qualities of the pick-ups used till that time, would reduce their main disadvantage : too great a sensitivity to the electric environment of the guitar.

The magnetic field of a single coil pick-up can actually capture not only the vibrations of the strings but also certain interference coming from neon lights or nearby electric motors, thus producing an undesirable hum.

Walter Fuller and Seth Lover got to work using the principle according to which two coils placed **in parallel** and **out-of-phase** would allow the vibrations coming from sources outside the guitar to be cancelled out while retaining only the signal coming from the vibration of the strings.

After about a year and a half of trials, the "Humbucking" pick-up, in other words

LES PAUL Junior (1956)

LES PAUL Special (1955)

Larry CORYELL.

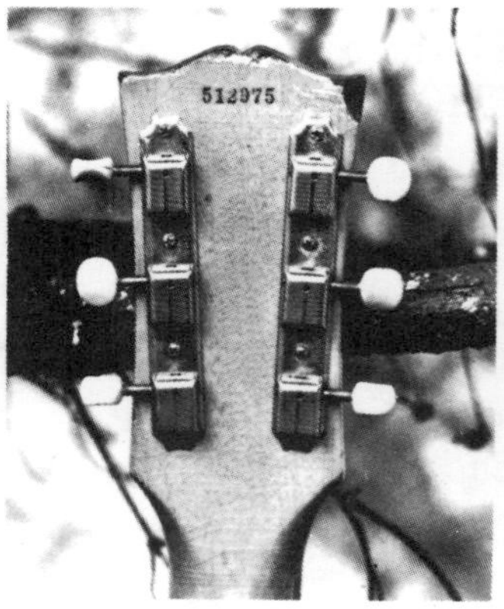


The Les Paul Special headstock... front and back: Note the six digit serial number and the "three on a plate" machine heads.

LES PAUL TV

The 1955/1957 edition of the Les Paul model with P-90 pick-ups and a Tune-O-Matic bridge.

Richard BETTS of the Allman Brothers Band playing a Gold-Top with humbuckers.

1958 Gold-Top with Humbucking pick-ups and Tune-O-Matic bridge. This fourth variant remained available for slightly more than a year.

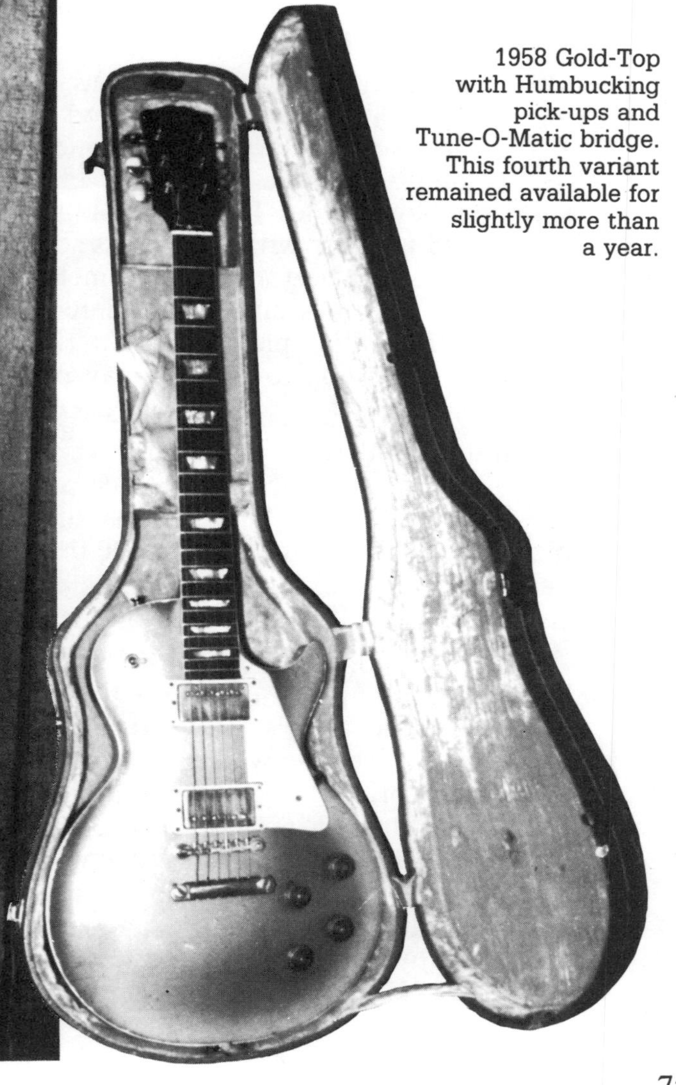

"bucking the hum" was perfected and consequently Seth Lover registered on June 22, 1955 a patent that was officially confirmed on July 28, 1959 (Patent Number 2896491).

The creation of this pick-up is, therefore, most often attributed to Seth Lover, who could have his design confirmed even though three patents had already been registered at the time on a similar subject, respectively by Lesti in 1936, Knoblaugh in 1938 and Russell in 1941. Nevertheless, as none of them referred exactly to the same application of a "Humbucking", pick-up, the patent was finally granted in 1959.

The "Humbucking" pick-up introduced at this time consisted in two black plastic bobbins having theoretically two 5,000 turn coils of number 42 plain enamel copper wire with a dark maroon insulation. An Alnico II or IV type magnet was placed under the two coils, one of which had adjustable poles although the initial patent drawing didn't have any. However, in line with its preceding pick-ups Gibson thought the adjustable poles were a strong selling point.

The six adjustable screws thread through the bobbin and a soft iron rod resting against the South side of the magnet whilst the six non adjustable poles were in contact with the North side. The two bobbins were firmly held in place with four brass screws on to a nickel silver bottom plate. A metal cover enveloped the unit and was soldered to this bottom plate to completely insulate the entire assembly according to the Faraday principle.

Though perfected as early as 1955, it was not until 1957 that the "Humbucking" pick-up was officially introduced to replace progressively the "P-90" or "Alnico" type single coil pick-ups on the most luxurious Gibson models. The new pick-up was designated under code name p.u. 490 in the Gibson files.

Until around the end of 1962, the "Humbucking" pick-ups mounted on the different Gibson electric models exhibited a small black decal, on which the words "**Patent Applied For**" were printed, even though the patent had been obtained in 1959 ! Then, starting at the end of 1962, a new decal showing a patent number was put on the bottom plate of the pick-ups. However, it seems that the number indicated by Gibson at the time i.e. patent Number 2737842 did not in fact correspond to the actual patent number obtained by Seth Lover for his "Humbucker". Apparently, Gibson hoped to "discourage" once again eventual copiers, previously threatened by the "patent applied for" label.

Until the end of the 1970's the Humbucking pick-ups placed in the "rhythm" and "lead" positions on the Gibson guitars showed no difference in their specifications.

It is useless to insist on the mystique that today surrounds the "Patent Applied For" Humbucking pick-ups, simply known as "**P.A.F.**", and many consider them to be the best pick-ups ever produced by Gibson. Nostalgia and a certain snob appeal, to be sure, play a part in such a statement, but nevertheless, it is undeniable that the original design has undergone over the years slight modifications which, altogether can in fact make a real difference in the sound.

Thus, what could be called the "**original Humbucking pick-up**", was characterized by a relatively weak Alnico magnet — Alnico II or IV — and two coils of 5,000 turns each.

Now, it looks as though, the winding machines Gibson had in the 1950's were, not fitted with an automatic stop counter and this does explain why there are so many variances in the older pick-ups.

For this reason, it appears that the coil of the first Humbucking pick-ups can vary considerably from one unit to the other. Certain pick-ups have up to twice 5,700 turns, and even, according to Gibson engineers twice 6,000 turns ! Naturally the DC resistance was modified and from 7.8 KΩ for a regular pick-up (2 × 5,000 turns), it can reach up to 9 KΩ for an overwound unit.

In another respect, when creating the Humbucking pick-up, Seth Lover (and Walter Fuller) had first resorted to using the magnets Gibson kept in stock for single coil pick-ups, in particular those known under the reference M-55, with the dimensions of 0.125" (h) × 0.500" ($\omega$) × 2.5" (L) In order to facilitate the mounting of the different components used in a Humbucking pick-up, Gibson starting around 1960, used a slightly smaller magnet — less long and less wide — designated M-56, which could have modified somewhat the tonal response. Later on the intensity of the Alnico magnets used for Humbuckers pick-ups actually reached grade V while the

Robert FRIPP with his Les Paul Custom

Keith RICHARDS of the Rolling Stones in concert.

"The Fretless Wonder"

THE INCOMPARABLE

LES PAUL CUSTOM GUITAR

Here is the ultimate in a solid body Gibson Electric Spanish Guitar—players rave about its extremely low, smooth frets and easy playing action, call it the "Fretless Wonder." Now with three humbucking, adjustable pickups, this new and improved "Les Paul Custom" guitar has increased power, greater sustaining and a clear, resonant, sparkling tone, with the widest range of tonal colorings. Finished in solid ebony color for rich contrast with the gold-plated metal fittings.

Solid Honduras mahogany body, graceful cutaway design with carved top; bound with alternating white and black strips • mahogany neck with exclusive Gibson Adjustable Truss Rod • bound, ebony fingerboard with deluxe pearl inlays • Three powerful, humbucking magnetic pickups • individually adjustable gold-plated polepieces • separate tone and volume controls • three-way toggle switch provides a new method of tone mixing: top position selects top pickup for rhythm; center position activates the center and lower picks simultaneously for extreme highs and special effects; lower position operates lower pickup for playing lead. Tailpiece can be moved up or down to adjust string tension • Tune-O-Matic bridge permits adjusting string action and individual string lengths for perfect intonation • gold-plated Sealfast individual machine heads with deluxe buttons • gold-plated metal end pin and strap holder. Padded leather strap included.

SPECIFICATIONS

12¾" wide, 17½" long, 1¾" thick, 24¾" scale, 22 frets

| | |
|---|---|
| **Les Paul Custom**—Ebony Finish | $375.00 |
| **No. 537 Case**—Faultless, gold plush lined | 47.50 |
| **No. ZC-CLP Zipper Case Cover** | 21.50 |

Excerpt from the 1958 catalog depicting the "incomparable" Les Paul Custom.

Les Paul Custom (1959)

number of turns was temporarily reduced during the 1960's, marking a new drift from the original design.

Lastly another important change around 1963 must be mentioned as it involves the quality of the wire. The gauge of the wire delivered to Gibson remained the same (number 42) but it was given an insulating sheath slightly thicker than before which had a fractional influence on the capacitance and the inductance. The "old" wire can be recognized by its dark marroon color while the "new" one is black. Furthermore it seems that Gibson also changed the way of winding its pick-ups at that time undoubtedly due to the adoption of new machines.

Be that as it may, these successive alterations did not come from a deliberate willingness of the company or its engineers to modify their pick-ups — especially to lower their quality or performance — but were brought about by the evolution of the component industry or by an improvement in the assembly procedures so as to obtain a product with a more consistent quality. Moreover it must be stated that Gibson did not appear to be immediately aware of the subtle modification in the quality of the wire it was supplied with... and when it had, what could happen ? The new wire almost had the same specifications as the former and it would have probably been accepted.

Because of these details there are "**several types**" of P.A.F. pick-ups, with distinct specifications... and without a doubt, some are certainly "better" than others (a subjective appraisal). Nonetheless, the mystique surrounding the P.A.F. pick-ups — as opposed the "non-P.A.F." pick-ups — is stronger than ever, to such a point that Gibson has introduced in 1980 an allegedly faithful re-edition of its original Humbucking pick-up !

Apart from the "Patent Applied For" decals which unfortunately have started recently to be counterfeited, a fully original P.A.F. pick-up can be identified thanks to :

1 - **the distinct square hole** with a ring around it, featured on the top and bottom of the bobbin. This original bobbin designed by Seth Lover was used until approximately 1967 when a change in tooling lead to the appearence of a new bobbin with a "T" on top ;

2 - **the dark maroon** color of the wire insulation and the black color of the two connected wires at the end of the bobbins (i.e. finish of adjustable coil + finish of non adjustable coil) Starting around 1963, the wire insulation appeared to be "blacker" and the two connected wires were white instead of black.

However it must noted that very early patent number pick-ups would exhibit such characteristics... but would also sound about the same for all matters ! In the last resort the size of the magnet could be of some help.

In 1957, the "Les Paul Model" received two Humbucking pick-ups in place of the single coil units with white plastic covers used since 1952. This fourth variant in the original series existed from around mid-1957 until mid-1958, or approximately a year. However it must be noted that a few Gold tops with white P-90's were shipped from the factory until 1958 (bearing 1958 serial numbers).

The other specifications, naturally, remained identical to the preceding versions, taking into account the evolution of the bridge tailpiece since 1952.

Some Les Paul "Gold Tops" of this period were made entirely of mahogany, without a maple top. This variation was probably due to a temporary shortage of maple or to the use of bodies initially intended for the production of Les Paul Custom. Unless one has a tremendously expert ear, or is in a position to compare side by side an all mahogany model with a regular Gold Top, the gold lacquer must be taken off before it can be actually realized.

A little later in 1957, the Les Paul Custom was in turn modified to receive three Humbucking pick-ups in place of the two single coil pick-ups used since 1954.

The preselection system of the pick-ups was obviously modified (without any aesthetic altering, though) as the three-position toggle switch of the new Custom model allowed to obtain successively :

1 - the pick-up near the neck ("front" pick-up) ;

2 - the pick-up near the bridge and the center pick-up together out of phase.

3 - the pick-up near the bridge (or "back" pick-up).

On this model it was not possible to select the middle pick-up alone, nor the three pick-ups altogether. Moreover the second option

A few "Patent Applied For" pick-ups resting on a Les Paul Standard. Note the small decal on the bottom plate, as well as the square hole with a ring on top of the bobbin.

Joe WALSH and Don FELDER of the Eagles with Tony DUKES. Joe Walsh and Don Felder are each holding a Standard while Tony Dukes exhibits one of the rare Customs fitted with only two humbucking pick-ups.

Some of the original
Les Paul Standards are
especially remarkable
thanks to their tiger
striped curly maple top.

Eric CLAPTON
and his "Sunburst" during
Cream's early days.

Les Paul
standard (1960)

can appear questionable as the selection of the center pick-up with the front pick-up instead of the back pick-up) would have been somewhat better. A "switchmaster" type wiring (see chapter 5) would have offered more versatility.

The guitar, however, kept the same appearance as before with two volume and tone controls acting on the pick-ups according to the selection. Some very rare Les Paul Custom guitars were produced with only **two** Humbucking pick-ups, but as this option was never shown in the catalogs of the period, they were probably built to special orders only. Like before, only the opaque black finish was available for this revised Les Paul Custom which systematically received in the late fifties, the new Grover Rotomatic tuning machines.

## THE LES PAUL STANDARD

In 1958, the "Les Paul Model" was modified again and this **fifth and last** variant of the original period is today the most sought after by enthusiasts of "old" Les Paul guitars... it is therefore one of the most expensive collectors'instrument that can be acquired on the "vintage" guitar market nowadays.

Compared to the 1957-1958 version, only the overall finish was changed as Gibson withdrew the "Gold Top" finish in use since 1952 for a striking "Cherry Sunburst" on top with the body and neck in cherry red. This new finish — cherry red into yellow — was offered at the time with no increase in price — still $ 247.50 in 1958 — and allowed the carved maple piece to be shown at its best for the first time. On the "**Sunburst**" (as they are now nicknamed) the top is made of two bookmatched pieces of maple, curly or "tiger striped", for the most beautiful effect. However, some Les Paul Standards were manufactured with a one piece curly maple top.

The intensity of the movements of the maple can also greatly vary from one guitar to another, determining to a large extent the present collection value of this instrument and its tremendous appeal. Thus some "Sunbursts" have a very faint curl, if no curl at all, whilst others have large even stripes from top to bottom.

In most cases the "Cherry Sunburst" finish has gently faded with age and the top has turned somewhat "orange" with the rest of the guitar becoming more of a natural mahogany color. We once came across a 1960 Standard on which a damaged spot in the varnish of the body had been mended quite invisibly by the owner with red paint to match the color of the guitar. As time passed by the red finish faded away but not the painted spot which is now clearly visible on the body !

The change in the finish of the "Les Paul Model", which, with this change became known as the "**Les Paul Standard**", was officially announced in the December 1958 issue of the "Gibson Gazette", the newsletter published by the company to introduce its new models, and to release articles on the different Gibson players. However, considering the number of 1958 "Sunburst" guitars in circulation, it is highly probable that the change was applied to the model much earlier, most certainly, around the summer of 1958.

For playing purposes it is interesting to note that starting in early 1960, the Les Paul Standard received a much flatter neck, which in fact was to remain characteristic on most Gibson models until about 1963.

It is paradoxical to note that the "Cherry Sunburst" Les Paul Standard did not show up in the March 1959 Gibson catalog — which was merely a reissue (with the exception of the color), of the March 1958 edition ! — and the model only appeared in the May 1960 catalog at the price of $ 265.00. A piece of advice to enthusiasts, beware of catalogs !

## THE LAST MODIFICATIONS

In 1958 — in the same December issue of the "Gibson Gazette" — the modification (much more radical) concerning the Les Paul Junior and "TV" was announced. Just like the "Standard", it is highly probable that the first "new style" Junior and TV guitars were put into production before the official announcement. In fact, it was rather a totally new model than a simple modification, since the traditional Les Paul single cutaway form was dropped and a double cutaway design introduced to allow for a completely free access to all the 22 frets. The body and neck were still

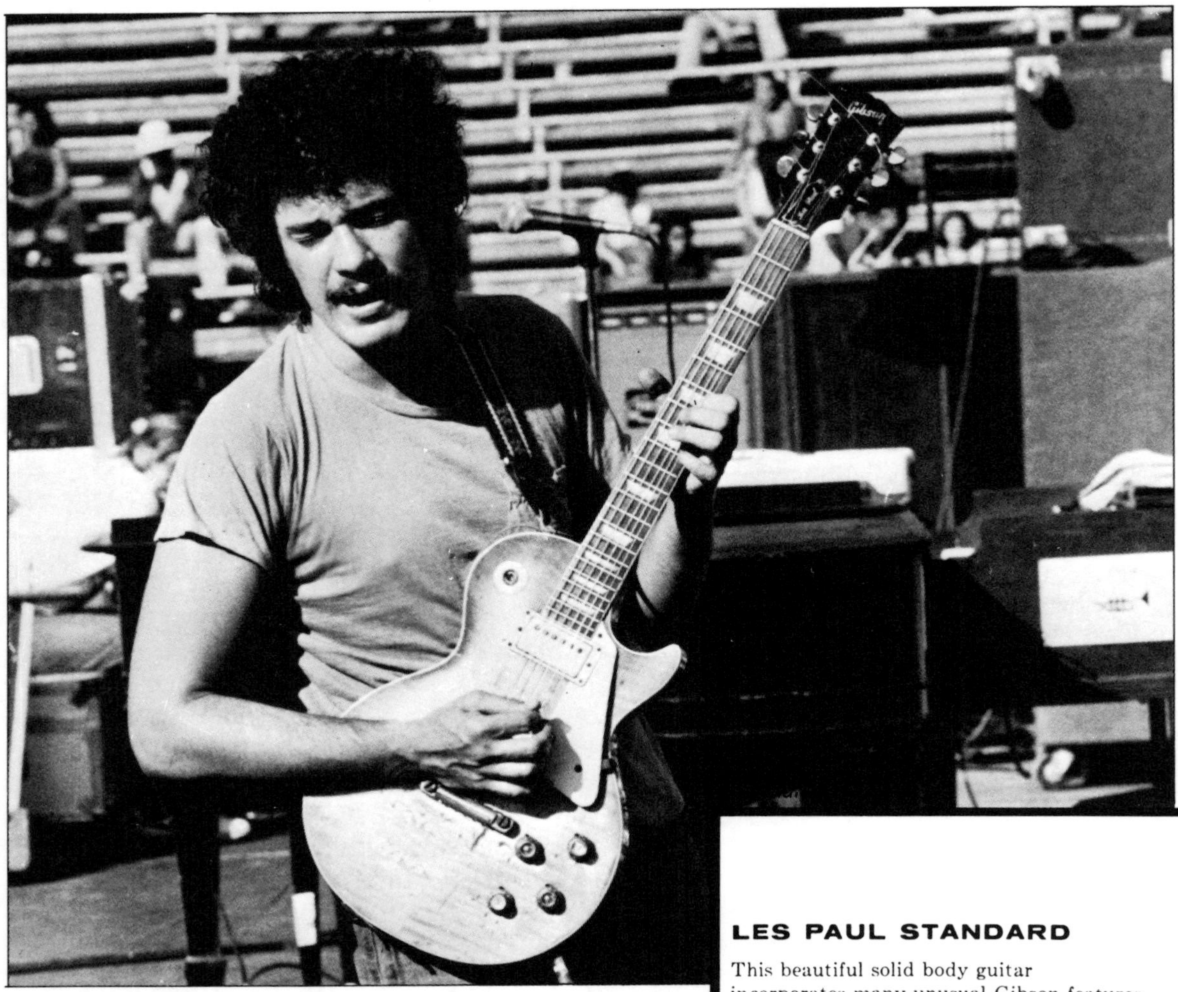

Mike BLOOMFIELD with the Les Paul Standard he used in the Electric Flag.

Excerpt from the 1960 catalog depicting the Les Paul Standard.

**LES PAUL STANDARD**

This beautiful solid body guitar incorporates many unusual Gibson features. Cherry sunburst carved maple top, mahogany body and neck. Combination bridge and tailpiece is a Gibson first. Tailpiece can be moved up or down to adjust tension. Tune-O-Matic bridge permits adjusting string action and individual string lengths. Finish in the striking cherry sunburst. Nickle-plated metal parts and individual machine heads with deluxe buttons. Deluxe padded leather strap included.

- Slim, fast, low-action neck—with exclusive extra low frets, joins body at 16th fret
- One-piece mahogany neck, adjustable truss rod
- Rosewood fingerboard, pearl inlays
- Graceful cutaway design
- Adjustable Tune-O-Matic bridge
- Twin powerful humbucking pickups with separate tone and volume controls which can be pre-set
- Three-position toggle switch to activate either or both pickups

12¾" wide, 17¼" long, 1¾" thin . . . 24¾" scale, 22 frets

**Les Paul Standard** Cherry sunburst finish **$265.00**

535 Faultless, plush-lined case $42.50

ZC-LP Deluxe zipper case cover $30.00

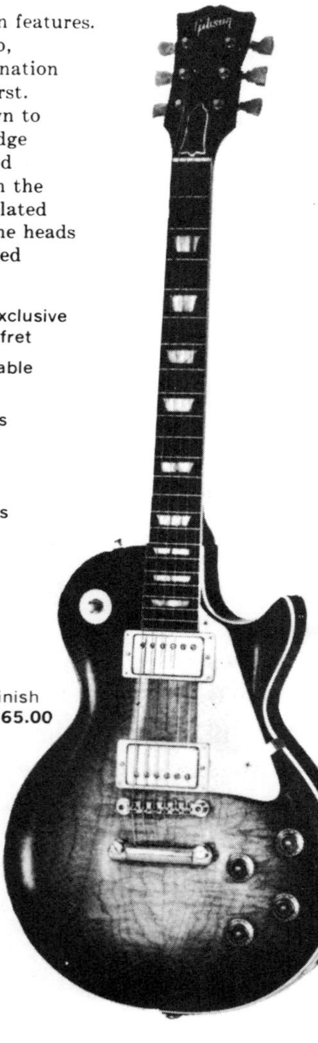

Owing to a lack of black pigment (?) a large number of humbucking pick ups were manufactured between 1959 and 1960 with double white or black and white bobbins. This 1960 Les Paul Standard is factory original with its black and white pick ups.

mahogany with an unbound rosewood fingerboard.

The pick-up and controls as well as the other electrical specifications remained unchanged. However, a "Cherry" finish that was not opaque replaced the former brown-into-yellow sunburst. It was the first commercial appearance of this finish which was progressively adopted by in increasing number of Gibson models, more particularly in the "SG" series starting in 1961. The new Junior was characterized by the easy access to the upper registers thanks to its entirely "free" fingerboard, since the neck joined the body beyond the 22nd fret.

The "TV" model underwent exactly the same alteration in shape while, naturally, keeping its characteristic yellow color which earned it the TV name. This finish, however, slightly evolved over the years from a rather "straw yellow" nuance to a sort of light "banana yellow".

Like the Les Paul Standard, the new Les Paul Junior and TV models did not appear in the 1959 catalog for the reasons we have mentioned, but only in the 1960 catalog.

The "3/4" version of the Les Paul Junior also received the new double cutaway form, but it remained characterized by a 19 fret fingerboard. The neck joined the body at the fifteenth fret only and therefore the fingerboard, did not provide a free access to the upper registers. All the other specifications remained unchanged.

In 1959, the Les Paul Special was brought into line with the Junior and TV models and fitted with the same double cutaway shape. The change was announced in the March-April issue of the 1959 "Gibson Gazette" which mentioned "Cherry Red" (like the Junior) or "Limed Mahogany" as available finishes. A few "Specials" were equally made with an opaque red finish.

The first double cutaway Les Paul Special guitars had the rhythm pick-up almost stuck against the fingerboard and the preselection switch located above the volume and tone controls of the front pick-up. Later on, the rhythm pick-up was moved back to strengthen the neck-to-body junction, and the 3-position toggle switch was placed in front of the volume controls right under the "stud" bridge. This second variant still offered full access to the 22 frets.

Starting in 1959, a "3/4" version of the double cutaway Les Paul Special was also commercialized and produced in fairly small quantities.

In the fashion of the "3/4" Junior model, this "Special" was characterized by a 19 fret fingerboard with the neck to body junction at the fifteenth fret.

On the various models exhibiting the new double cutaway shape, the edges were more or less rounded according to the batches. Some "Juniors" or "Specials" showed a sharper (or less rounded) edges than others. Likewise owing to the difference in the feel of the necks between 1958 and 1961, the heel of the double cutaway Les Pauls can vary to a rather large extent.

In 1959, a small shortage of black plastic meant that some coils of the Humbucking pick-ups were made out of **cream**-colored plastic. Thus between 1959 and 1960, the pick-ups most often had two black coils, but some pick-ups had two cream-colored bobbins, or even one black and one cream-colored. Naturally these different pick-ups are technically identical... but the full white or black and white bobbins (nicknamed "Zebra") are much rarer.

In 1960, the "Les Paul Special" and the "Les Paul TV" became respectively the "**SG Special**" and the "**SG TV**", without any change in their specifications. However, with the loss of the Les Paul name, the "SG Special" and "SG TV" naturally lost the "Les Paul" markings on the peg-head.

However the two models are most often assimilated with the Les Paul range and in any case rarely called by their real name, i.e. "SG" (Solid Guitar), more willingly reserved for the new double cutaway series introduced in early 1961.

# THE END OF THE ORIGINAL LES PAUL SERIES

As paradoxical as it may seem today, the popularity of the Les Paul guitars had not ceased to wane over the 1950's. The shipping statistics clearly show a drop beginning in 1956, somewhat countered by the arrival of guitars between 1958 and 1959 so as to curb the fall.

This fall absolutely unbelievable for anyone today, was due, at the time, to an "internal" competition from new models introduced by Gibson since 1952 — particularly the semi-solid or the thin-line guitars — but also to the rivalry of a few Californian manufacturers (Fender or Rickenbacker)...

One can equally imagine that the Les Paul Standard or Custom, in spite of the modifications they underwent, were no longer, as far as the aesthetics or the sound were concerned in gear with the aspirations of the guitarists of the early sixties.

At the end of 1960, Gibson took the decision to proceed with a complete overhauling of its Les Paul line which lead to the introduction in early 1961, of the new sharp double cutaway versions which took the SG name by the end of 1963.

Theoretically, all the "original" Les Paul line was still available at the beginning of 1961, either with serial numbers applied with a rubber stamp (e.g. Les Paul Custom, number 1-1055) or with serial numbers imprinted in the wood on the back of the headstock (e.g. Les Paul Custom, number 6508). However, we have never found, to this day, an old style "Sunburst" Les Paul Standard with a 1961 serial number, whereas Customs, Juniors and Specials of this same year can easily be found.

According to the Gibson's books in Kalamazoo, the very last original Les Paul guitars were registered as late as October 1961 (Les Paul Special "3/4"). At this time the first SG/Les Paul guitars had already been introduced, and the change in the Les Paul line announced. As a matter of fact, during a couple of months in the early part of 1961, the "old" and the "new" models were both available.

It is useless today to insist on the value, soundwise or moneywise, of the "old" Les Paul guitars, that musicians such as Eric Clapton or Mike Bloomfield were going to use with so much success that Gibson decided seven years later, in 1968, to reintroduce the series in its original, single cutaway form. In the same way, it would be too long to draw up the list of all the guitarists with a reputation playing an old "Standard", a "Gold Top" or even a "Custom". Let us simply cite some among the most famous : Al DiMeola, Jimmy Page, Jeff Beck, Joe Walsh, Duane Allmann, J. Geils, Billy Gibbons, Charlie Daniels, Richard Betts, Robert Fripp, Mick Taylor, Steve Hàckett...

## CHRONOLOGICAL EVOLUTION OF THE LES PAUL MODELS

1951 The Gibson "solid body" guitar prototype is adopted by Les Paul.

1952 Introduction of the first "Les Paul" guitar with Les Paul's combination trapeze bridge-tailpiece (first variant).

1953 The "Les Paul Model" is modified to receive a "stud" tailpiece (second variant).

1954 Introduction of the "Les Paul Custom" and the "Les Paul Junior". The first "Les Paul TV" guitars are released.

1955 Introduction of the "Les Paul Special". The "Les Paul Model" is modified to receive a "Tune-O-Matic" bridge (third variant).

1956 Introduction of the "3/4" version of the "Les Paul Junior".

1957 The "Les Paul Model" is equipped with Humbucking pick-ups (fourth variant). The "Les Paul Custom" is also equipped with these new pick-ups, but receives three of them.

1958 The "Les Paul Model" becomes "Les Paul Standard" and loses its gold top finish in favor of a "Cherry Sunburst" finish (fifth variant). The "Les Paul Junior" and "TV" receive a new double cutaway form. Introduction of a "3/4" version of the "Les Paul Special".

1959 The "Les Paul Special", in turn, receives the new double cutaway form. Introduction of a "3/4" version of the "Les Paul Special" with double cutaway.

1960 The "Les Paul Special" becomes the "SG Special". The "Les Paul TV" becomes the "SG TV".

1961 The original "Les Paul" series is withdrawn and replaced by a new sharp double cutaway model later to be known as the SG series.

Les Paul Junior "3/4" (1960)

top : Les Paul Special "3/4"
Note the neck-to-body junction at the $15^{th}$ fret and the recessed position of the stud tailpiece.

bottom : close-up view of the heel on the double cutaway models introduced by Gibson in 1958.

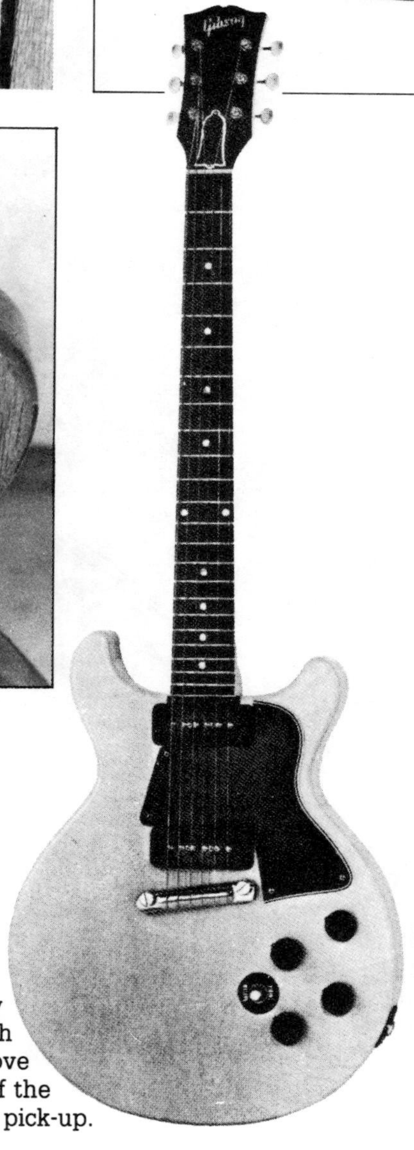

Les Paul Special (1959) in double cutaway form. This is the first variant with the toggle switch located above the volume and tone controls of the rhythm pick-up.

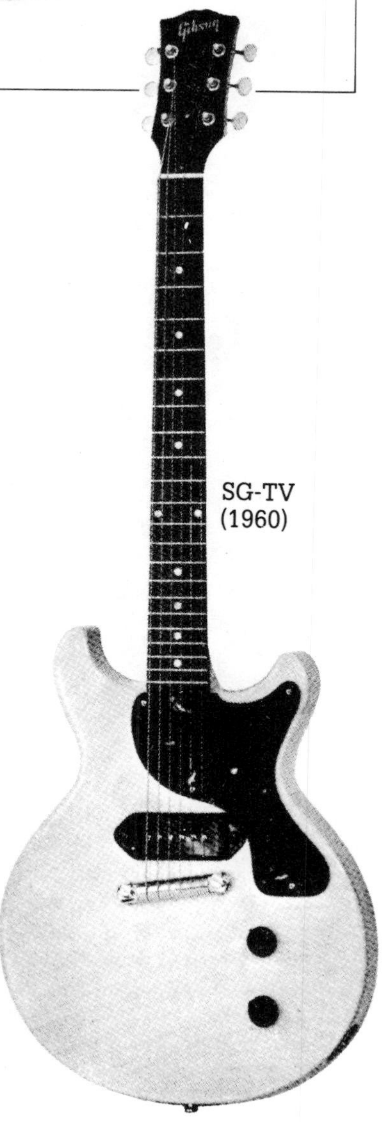

SG-TV (1960)

The first and the last Les Paul Model...

This document assembles the first and the last production Les Paul models (or Std) originally released by Gibson.
On the left is a Les Paul model with P-90 single coil pick-ups and a trapeze combination bridge tail-piece.
Besides this 1953 edition is finished all gold — or solid gold — as it was sometimes the case in the early fifties.
On the right is a very unusual Les Paul Standard with humbuckers, lacquered with a glossy cherry red finish.
Its serial number is 0-9350, albeit in slightly taller digits than regular in those days. However it looks as though this particular model, of which only a handful are known to exist, was actually shipped in the early sixties,
presumably because a few left over bodies had been found somewhere at the factory
after the cherry sunburst Les Paul Std had been discontinued in 1960.
(guitars courtesy of Robb Lawrence).

# CHAPTER 4

# THE OTHER SOLID BODY GUITARS OF THE 1950's

After officially introducing its first "solid body" electric in 1952, Gibson was to offer a growing number of this type of instrument in the 1950's. The "Les Paul" line was the subject of the preceding chapter and now we will examine the "other" Solid Bodies of this period.

## THE EB-1 ELECTRIC BASS

Hardly a year after the appearance of the first "Les Paul" guitar in 1952, Gibson commercialized — once again in response to its young Californian rival — an electric bass in 1953.

This 4-string bass was characterized by its "violin" shape which, at first glance, makes it immediately recognizable.

The body was made from a block of mahogany, sculpted in the form of a violin, and on which an artificial sound hole, as well as a double purfling outlining the contours, were painted on. The neck was made of a single piece of mahogany with a 20 fret unbound rosewood fingerboard featuring pearl dot position markers. The scale length has been set at 30 1/2" (i.e. a scale shorter than the Fender bass of that time) making it easier to play for a guitarist. In another respect, the very form of this bass greatly facilitated the access to the treble end. The peg-head carried the Gibson insignia inlaid in pearl, without the crown design or any inscription indicating the type of instrument. Kluson banjo-like tuning machines, were used and the strings were attached to a one-piece bridge-tailpiece, which did not allow the intonation to be set string by string. However, this preset bridge could be vertically adjusted at either end, like on a Les Paul Junior for example.

The pick-up on the first Gibson electric bass was rather particular as it had according to Walt Fuller nearly 25,000 turns !... (enough to obtain a rather devastating bass sound !) in only one "horizontal" coil .This square shaped pick-up was equipped with a brown bakelite cover, and the magnets were placed at the extremity located at the end of the fingerboard, while the adjustable poles, mounted perpendicular to the polar mass, appeared on the side of the pick-up facing the bridge.

A volume and a tone controls completed the assembly.

This "enormous" coil was split in two at a later date all the while keeping the same number of turns, and the adjustable poles were placed in the middle of the pick-up.

One of the most amusing aspects of this electric bass, retrospectively, concerns the adaptable extension-pin that was delivered with the instrument so that it could be played standing up like a real double-bass. Undoubtedly this was the reason why it had a "violin" shape intended, in all logic, to favor its assimilation with the instrument that it was supposed to replace.

This new instrument was originally called the "**Electric Bass**", and it was not until 1958 that the "violin bass" took the desi-

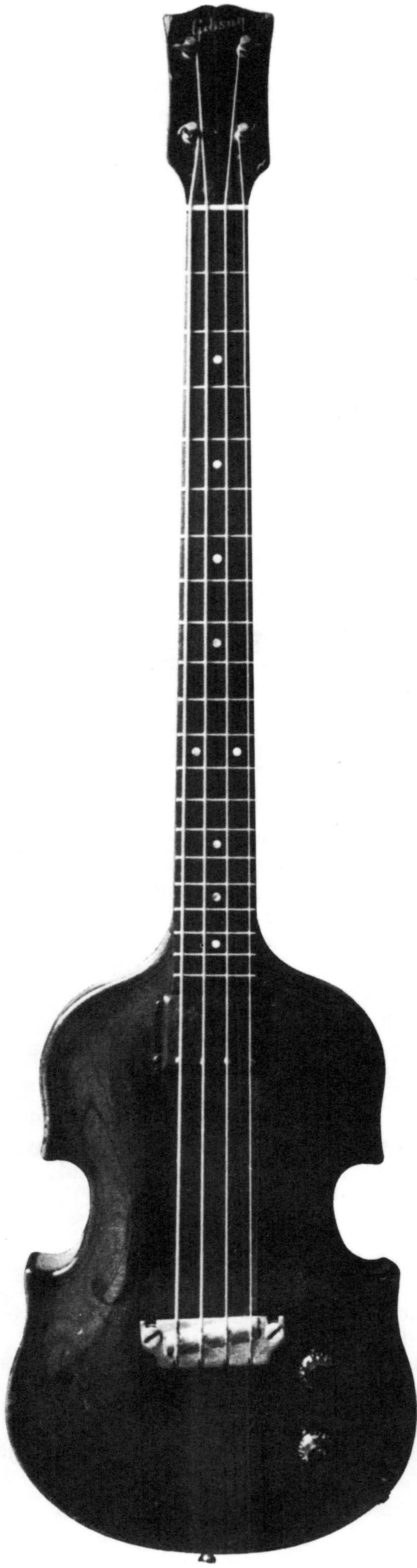

EB-1 (1956)...
Gibson's first electric bass.

The Kluson banjo-like machine heads used on the EB-1.

Close-up view of the electric bass pick-up with its pole-pieces on the edge of the cover facing the bridge.

gnation **EB-1** because of the introduction of "another" bass in the Gibson catalog (the EB-2 semi-solid bass).

In the early fifties, the production of an instrument such as the electric bass took off quite nicely, then the rhythm slowed down starting in 1956 until the complete discontinuation of the model in 1958, and the appearance of new basses such as the semi-solid EB-2 in 1958 and the solid body EBO in 1959.

The inaccuracy of certain Gibson catalogs must be pointed out one more time as the EB-1 was shown in the 1959 edition, whereas the last ones were actually manufactured and shipped in 1958.

The EB-1 was the object of a re-edition in 1970 probably more out of nostalgia than for the intrinsic qualities of the instrument which, however, has a certain interest for collectors.

# THE "MODERNISTIC" GUITARS

A few years later, Gibson offered some aesthetically speaking radical solid body guitars, whose very great renown today equals only the obscurity they met at the time of their introduction !

The "**Modernistic**" **guitars** — this is the name used in the Gibson price list of July 1, 1958 — are nowadays among the most controversial and the most... covetted electric guitars in the history of the company. This is why we will try to understand really what these "extraordinary" guitars were and how they came about.

Around 1955, Gibson decided that it was time to end the widespread idea that Gibson was too traditional even a little "old-fashioned", at a time when Rock and Roll was making its first inroads. Fantastic strides were then achieved in all fields, and Gibson guitars were perhaps not reflecting enough this progress, while certain Californian competitors (you no doubt guessed who !) were ably using it to their advantage in order to titillate the public interest.

After hearing the recriminations of several Gibson dealers, who themselves got remarks from salesmen or customers, Ted Mac Carty was irritated to the point that he undertook "to show them what Gibson could do" and started working on something really "wild and unusual !"

A few designers were therefore invited to Kalamazoo with the mission of creating, in collaboration with the Gibson R & D department, shapes as radically innovative as possible.

The first objective was unquestionably to look "different" and "modern"... there would be time later on to see if the drawings could turn into a prototype which would be manufactured with the equipment and the machines of the factory. A hundred sketches of so were thus conceived, with all sorts of weird shapes among which a dozen were selected by Gibson to move on to the prototype stage.

The story then gets a little complicated and the opinions begin to diverge slightly among the protagonists of the time we have talked to. As a matter of fact, three of four models were chosen among the prototypes created, to be introduced at a trade show. At this stage, it must absolutely be pointed out that none of the prototypes appeared to be given an official designation.

The final names of the instruments were then generally "coined" by the sales force located in Chicago (otherwise known as CMI) and not at the factory, where only "nicknames" were given to such and such a prototype in the process of being manufactured. Three or four forms thus materialized among which was the future "Flying V".

The **Flying V** is in fact the easiest model to identify thanks to its shape, and consequently, it is the guitar people remember the most. Initially, the "Flying V", which was apparently a personal idea of Ted Mac Carty, was a triangular-shaped guitar with a rounded base. Unfortunately created as such, it seems that it was found too heavy and it had to be slightly altered... or emptied out at the back end, hence the famous arrow symbol which quickly won it the nickname, then the name "Flying V" (or Flying Arrow as certain sources indicate).

The other prototypes were given nicknames clearly denoting the modern and

An original FLYING V fitted with a black scratch plate. The corrugated pad used to prevent the inst.ument from sliding off in the seated position is quite visible on the right wing.

| | | |
|---|---|---|
| Les Paul Jr. | Guitar, Solid Body Cutaway, with built-in pickup | 120.00 |
| 115 | Durabilt Case for above | 13.50 |
| | **MODERNISTIC GUITARS** | |
| Explorer | Guitar, Solid Body | $247.50 |
| Flying V | Guitar, Solid Body | 247.50 |
| | Case for above models | 75.00 |
| | **ELECTRIC SPANISH GUITARS (Cutaway)** | |
| ES-175 | Guitar, Cutaway—Sunburst Finish | $235.00 |
| ES-175N | Guitar, Cutaway—Natural Finish | 250.00 |
| ES-175D | Special Guitar, Cutaway—Sunburst, two built-in pickups | 290.00 |
| ES-175DN | Special Guitar, Cutaway—Natural, | |

Excerpt from the Gibson price list dated July 1, 1958.

futuristic character of Gibson's attempt. The most commonly cited names referring to these models were "**Futura**", "**Futurama**", "**Futuristic**", "**Moderne**", "**Modernistic**", "**Explorer**", "**Discoverer**".

Three (according to Mr. Bellson) or four prototypes (according to Mr. Mac Carty) were exhibited by Gibson during various conventions around 1957 after the designs had been kicked around the factory for at least two years. The guitars were all made of an African wood similar to mahogany, but whiter, called "Limba" and the pieces selected for the new models took the name "Korina".

The choice of such a material was brought about by Gibson's intention to use a clear wood, which could give the instrument a "natural" look with a simple coat of varnish. Maple being much too dense — and consequently too heavy — korina was quickly adopted, for it allowed Gibson not to bleach mahogany like on the Les Paul Special, while retaining very similar properties.

The reaction of the "professionals" towards these prototypes was at the same time one of scepticism and naturally of... bewilderment. Gibson had, to be sure, succeeded in shaking off its old image, even in shocking, but it had not exactly convinced, in so far as these new models were not really taken seriously by salesmen or even by the public.

Nevertheless, two models were soon put into production by Gibson.

At first, the "Flying V" was offered in the catalog dated March 25, 1958 as a "design of the future" at the price of $ 247.50 plus $ 75.00 for the case. The first production "V"'s were most probably started around the end of 1957.

Then under the "Modernistic Guitars" reading Gibson offered two models, the Explorer and the Flying V, both at the price of $ 247.50 plus case for $ 75.00 in its list of July 1, 1958. The sales department of CMI with Clarence Havenga at its head had undoubtedly reckoned that two "avant-garde" guitars were more than enough for Gibson's needs.

As for the other prototypes, they were **never** offered to the public as regular models, nor even manufactured in quantity.

From what we could find out from the Gibson documents, and from interviews with people like Ted Mac Carty or Julius Bellson, the other "forms" never went beyond the prototype stage.

# ABOUT THE MODERNE

The "**Moderne**", no doubt, existed as a sketch, then as a "prototype" among the twelve models or so that were made between 1955 and 1957, but, in our opinion, it was never actually produced in quantity like the Explorer or the Flying V.

The ambiguity concerning the "Moderne" stems from the existence of a drawing shown in the patents submitted on June 20, 1957 by Ted Mac Carty (and officially confirmed on January 7, 1958). These patents were, at the time, registered for what was supposed to become the "Flying V", the "Explorer" and the "Moderne". On the other hand, the shipping records that we were able to consult in Kalamazoo actually show that 19 "Modernes" were shipped in 1958 and 3 in 1959. Consequently, for many, the "Moderne" did exist as a regular model.

*A drawing of the Moderne as outlined in the patent submitted by Ted Mac Carty in 1957*

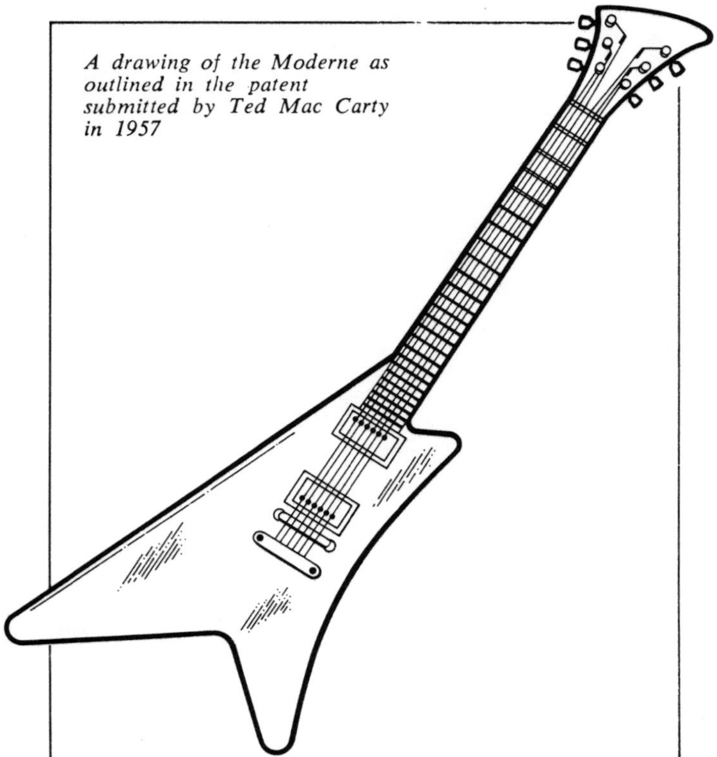

However, on second thought, it is rather strange to realize that no one has recently seen a "Moderne"... even the most reputable vintage dealers, even the craftiest and wealthiest specialists in collector's items in the United States or elsewhere, have never seen a single "Moderne" nor met someone of good faith who has held one (and let us be precise, be competent enough to know that it was not a fake !).

What is more, it is quite surprising, considering, the very high assessment value that the "Flying V" or "Explorer" have had on the collection instrument market for many years (... several thousands Dollars !) that no one has ever dreamt of trading a "Moderne" whose price would naturally soar up to unprecedented heights !!!

In another respect, 22 "Moderne" guitars is a lot... and so, at least a few should have "turned up" if only because of the price some would be willing to pay in order to have one. But it is also too few... In fact, at this time at Gibson, guitars were usually manufactured in batches of 40, and even though incidents during the manufacturing process could sometimes eliminate a few units, more than 22 should have been completed. Of course, if an instrument does not sell, the remaining samples can be sold to Gibson employees at a reduced price, or eventually destroyed or even kept for experimental purposes. Nevertheless, 18 out of 40 represents a substantial proportion, especially since at Gibson, wasting wood is not the usual habit.

In connection with this, it is curious to state that the shipping totals of such a "rare" model like the "Moderne" are accurately known, while those of a much more identified instrument such as the Explorer are somewhat "cloudy". As a matter of fact, the statistics concerning the exact number of Explorers shipped are not mentioned in the records we were able to consult.

Now, one must not forget that the Explorer and the Flying V were both introduced as "Modernistic Guitars" and from "Moderne" to "Modernistic" there is only one step !... more especially as the name "Modernistic Guitar" did not appear until 1958, at about the same time as the Explorer.

The "Modernes" shown in the Gibson records might be, in fact, Explorers ! However, according to various sources of information in the United States those "22" Modernes would actually represent the 22 experimental models designed by Gibson when the company toyed with the "Modernistic guitar" concept. After CMI decided to market only the Flying V and the Explorer, the factory would have shipped the other prototypes since the future of the series was not so bright... there was no reason for keeping the doomed modernistic guitars at home !

Undoubtedly some prototypes able to claim the "Moderne" designation have existed, but no stock model was ever manufactured under this name, which is not shown in any Gibson document intended for the public such as catalogs, price lists or "Gibson Gazettes". Now where are those prototypes or how many are they, are two very difficult questions to answer today. It is possible that a few "real" Modernes were among the 22 guitars shipped from the factory in 1958 and 1959, with other rarities. So far the only Modernes to have surfaced in the last few years were undeniably forgeries according to the people who had a chance to look at them.

May be one day a "real" Moderne will see the light of day ? (... in which case a photo to the author of this book is most welcome !).

Be that as it may, it must be known that Gibson frequently creates what Ted Mac Carty calls "Mavericks" — in other words, original models in the prototype state without any official designation — that can perfectly remain without any follow-up. As far as we can gather, the "Moderne" was one of these "Mavericks" !

# THE FLYING V AND THE EXPLORER

After this somewhat controversial paragraph on the "Moderne", let us examine more closely the characteristics of these two rare birds known as the Flying V and the Explorer.

The Flying V body.
These pictures clearly evidence the two symetrical wings
of Korina wood used on the original issue.
Note the holes on the back intended for the strings.

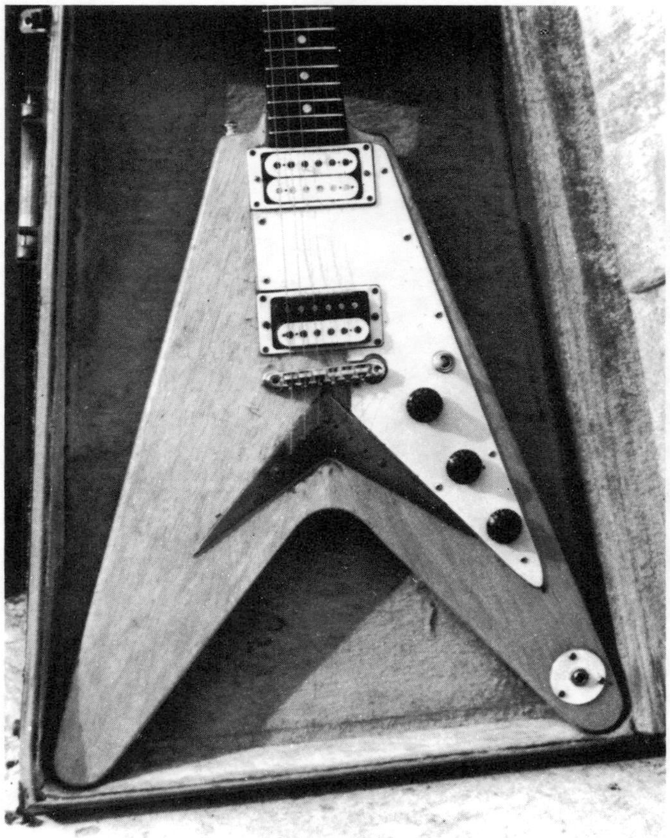

Billy Gibbons of ZZ Top.

J. GEILS with his modified Flying V.

This original issue Explorer belongs to the few guitars shipped in the early sixties. Note the plastic inserts on the Tune-O-Matic bridge and the silver capped knobs.

This original Explorer has been set up with a Bigsby Vibrato tailpiece.

The "**Flying V**" was the first "Modernistic" guitar to be offered in 1958 to the public. As already mentioned the body and the neck were made of Korina, while the unbound fingerboard was of rosewood with pearl dot position markers. The veins of the wood clearly show that the body was made from two symetrical wings glued to the extension of the neck, and not of a single piece of timber.

The "Flying V" was equipped with two (P.A.F.) Humbucking pick-ups with a volume control for each pick-up and a master tone control, whereas the preselection of the pick-ups was made by a traditional 3-position toggle switch. The strings were to be strung in the back of the guitar, then passed through a metal V-shaped tailpiece, before resting on a "Tune-O-Matic" bridge. All the metal parts were gold-plated, while the scratch plate bearing the controls was most often white, but also black. The out-put jack was placed in the lower half of the "V". Lastly, a corrugated rubber film was also attached on the edge of the lower half of the "V" to keep the guitar from sliding off in the sitting position.

Some details may have varied from one guitar to another on the early "V's", for the series had just been launched, however, the original 1958/59 issue of the Flying "V" is characterized by the following :

— the body is made of two symetrical pieces of Korina wood,
— the fingerboard features full access to all 22 frets,
— the neck joins the body, slightly beyond the 20th fret and the neck block is glued to the body on three sides,
— the three volume and tone controls are in a straight line,
— the "Patent Applied For" Humbucking pick-ups have an individual black plastic surrounding,
— the scratch plate only covers the bottom half of the body,
— the strings are strung in the back before passing through a "V-shaped" metal tailpiece,
— the Gibson logo is made of raised plastic letters and not pearl inlaid.

The original model was offered only with a "Natural" finish, otherwise yellow ochre, in a brown pink-lined rectangular case (see color picture).

The Flying V was not very successful in 1958, to such a point that certain retailers bought it as an attraction for their shop... like a sort of arrow indicating that they were selling Gibson guitars... but they did not try to sell the instrument itself.

The plant records indicate that 81 "V's" were shipped in 1958 and 17 in 1959, hence a total of 98 for those two years. In fact, it can logically be estimated that 3 batches of approximately 40 units were produced at the time. The rest of the last batch was then stored at the factory before subsequently being shipped at the beginning of the 1960's.

These later Flying V's can have, either an inked-on serial number corresponding to the actual period of their manufacture, or, if it was in the process of being made, a 5/6 digit number imprinted in the wood at the back of the headstock.

We were able to note in the Gibson ledgers that a Flying V with the serial number 9-1704 (= 1959) was registered on July 18, 1962. The "Flying V" guitars left aside in 1959 were accordingly shipped between 1962 and 1963. They are most often considered as original, even though their metal parts are nickel-plated (and not gold-plated), and the Humbuckers are no longer "Patent Applied For's". Lastly, their case was still rectangular, but black with a yellow plush lining.

The **Explorer** was introduced shortly after the Flying V with identical specifications, such as a Korina body and neck, two Humbucking pick-ups with two volume controls and one master tone control, a 22 fret unbound rosewood fingerboard with pearl dot position markers, a "Natural" finish and a price of $ 247.50 on July 1, 1958.

The Explorer, however, was fitted from the beginning with a stop tailpiece similar to the one mounted on the Les Paul guitars of that time, and consequently it never had the strings strung throught the body like the Flying V. The out-put jack was located on the rim while it was usually on the front for the Flying V.

Nevertheless, it can be said without hesitation, that the "Flying V" and the "Explorer" were two expressions of one identical concept !

Only the shape (and... the sound !) differentiated the "V" from its fellow modernistic guitar. The very first Explorers had a "V-shaped" peg-head similar to the one featured on the drawing used for the patent in 1957, with two rows of three tuning machines on each side of the V.

On this variant, the Gibson logo consisted in raised plastic letters stuck on the peg-head like on the "Flying V". A little later, the Explorer adopted the "Scimitar" headstock with all the tuning machines on one side and the Gibson logo inlaid in pearl.

As we said before, the exact number of Explorers actually made is not officially known for sure. However, at the time of the introduction of a reissue of the Explorer in 1976, Gibson made it clear that only 38 originals were actually made, namely one "batch". Taking into account the few samples known to have been shipped (like the Flying V) around 1962 and 1963, it is possible that a second batch of 40 guitars, was put into production but at the present, rather hard to verify, and for this reason, we will stick to the figure of 38 units indicated by Gibson. Besides, there can be some confusion with the statistics of the "Moderne", 19 of which were shipped (according to the Gibson ledgers) in 1958 and 3 in 1959 (this does not mean that they did have a 1959 number though !).

As regards the Explorers shipped in the early sixties, a few details can actually distinguish them from the 1958 original issue such as :

1) "Patent Number" pick-ups instead of "Patent Applied For's".

2) Plastic inserts on the Tune-O-Matic bridge instead of metal ones.

3) Silver-capped black knobs instead of uncapped gold ones.

At any rate it appears that Explorers were shipped in larger quantities than "Flying V's" at that time (hence a second batch ?) thanks to the introduction of the new Firebird series which resembled a "smoothed out" Explorer !

Besides the regular Explorer model, Gibson also made, on a custom order basis only, a few Explorer bass models. According to the different people we have consulted in the United States, it looks as though at least three Explorer basses were manufactured around 1959. Two of them were in the natural-looking Korina finish while the third one is remembered with a sunburst finish. The Explorer bass consisted of an Explorer guitar body fitted with an EB-2 type neck and electronics. In New York, we came across one of these exceedingly rare models whose story is truely "colorful" ! This 1959 Explorer Bass was originally custom ordered from Gibson by a musician named Roger Troy.

Unfortunately, for some reason he did not pick-up the instrument when it was delivered and it was bought then, by Wayne Bullock who played bass with Lonnie Mack. At that time it was finished in Natural (like a regular Explorer) with a brown plastic pick-up cover like the early EB-2. The bass was used on several Memphis recordings, then later on it was allegedly painted green (!) then blue (!!!) before being restored to its original condition by Robb Lawrence. The Explorer bass was subsequently sold to Johnny Winter's bass player Randy Hobbs and later found its way on to New York 48th street !... At least this is how the story goes ! In any case it clearly shows that several one-of-kind models made by Gibson did see the light of day even though they were never mentioned in a catalog or even offered as such to the public. Still, they are definitely Gibson electrics. Unfortunately it is impossible to take them all into account in this book, since nobody knows exactly how many "rare birds" like this were put together by the Gibson Custom department.

As everyone knows today, the Flying V and Explorer were later on to avenge the fate that overwhelmed them at the time of their introduction... In fact in order to buy an original "V" or Explorer nowadays one has to be relatively wealthy, to say the least ! Among the "fortunate" owners of a Flying V, we can find Billy Gibbons, J. Geils, Neil Young as well as blues player Albert King, while Eric Clapton and Rick Derringer were associated with the Explorer.

Once again, Gibson was too advanced for the tastes of the time !

The "scimitar" headstock of the Explorer.

The very early Explorers were fitted with such a "V" shaped headstock built along the lines of Ted Mac Carty's patent drawings. Note the Gibson logo in raised plastic letters like on the Flying V.

Explorer bass... custom made in the late fifties.

Early Explorer with a "V" shaped headstock. This particular instrument bears serial number 8-2142.

# THE EBO AND MELODY MAKER MODELS

In 1958, Gibson decided to replace the "violin" bass whose sales had not ceased to decline. As an inspiration for the new model Gibson chose the double cutaway shape used to "renovate" the Les Paul Junior, TV and later the Special. The production of the EB-1 was therefore discontinued in 1958, and the first EB-O basses were shipped in 1959.

The **EB-O** took on some of the EB-1's characteristics, such as a mahogany body and neck, a 20 fret unbound rosewood fingerboard with a 30 1/2" scale length, Kluson banjo like tuning machines and even the "fat" bass pick-up with the adjustable pole pieces now moved in the middle of the cover. The one piece neck joined the body beyond the seventeenth fret (!).

Besides the body shape, the EB-0 also adopted the same cherry red finish as the Les Paul Junior with a large pick-guard covering the lower half of the instrument. The EB-0 was to keep this thick double cutaway form until 1961 when the new thin double cutaway design, perfected for the Les Paul series, was extended to most of the "solid body" guitars and basses.

In 1959, Gibson introduced a new "economy" model destined for the least well-off fraction of solid body guitar enthusiasts since one of the keys of the Gibson policy has always been to offer a quality instrument in as wide a price range as possible.

Starting in 1959, the first fruits of a growing demand for electric guitars began to be harvested, and new instruments were added to complete the range, whereas the Kalamazoo plant was enlarged to house a bigger production.

Gibson's decision, under these circumstances, to offer a "solid body" model less expensive than a Les Paul Junior appeared, therefore, perfectly logical (even more so as the Japanese competition did not exist at the time).

This new model took the "**Melody Maker**" name and was available from 1959, both in a regular and in a "3/4" version, at the same price of $ 99.50.

The Melody Maker was made entirely of mahogany and had a one-piece body and neck, with an unbound rosewood fingerboard. It took on the form and dimensions of the original single cutaway Les Paul Junior (12 3/4" × 17 1/4"), but it was somewhat thinner at 1 3/8" compared to 1 3/4". Like a Les Paul, the neck joined the body at the 16th fret. The volume and tone controls, the out-put jack as well as the single pick-up located near the stud bridge were all attached onto a black plastic scratch-plate screwed on the body with the words "Melody Maker" in white letters at the end of the fingerboard.

The single coil pick-up was of new design without adjustable pole-pieces and featured a black plastic cover. On the very first Melody Makers, this pick-up had a wider coil with more turns while subsquently it was reduced and became narrower.

The Melody Maker was characterized by an exceptionally straight and narrow headstock for a Gibson, which nevertheless retained the classic design with a "moustache". The Gibson logo was applied thanks to a golden decal and not pearl inlaid for such a low priced model. Naturally the Kluson tuning machines were in two rows of 3 keys each with white oval plastic buttons as on the Les Paul Junior.

The finish was also similar to the original single cutaway Les Paul Junior with a brown-into-yellow sunburst on top and a dark mahogany shade on the rest of the body and neck.

Starting in 1960, a two-pick-up version was introduced as the "**Melody Maker D**" at the price of $ 135.00. Compared to the single-pick-up version, the MM-D received a second pick-up located at the end of the fingerboard with a set of volume and tone, control and a 3-position toggle switch.

Very quickly, the two Melody Maker models dropped their original form with a single cutaway, to adopt starting in 1961 a new double cutaway design. In fact this new version, which was produced until around early 1964, can be compared to a Melody Maker that would have been given a second cutaway perfectly symetrical to the first one.

EB-O (1959)

Melody Maker (1959)

1961 Melody Maker with its symetrical double cutaway shape.

The typically narrow headstock of the Melody Maker.

The Melody Maker was equipped with a unique single coil pick-up without adjustable pole pieces.

However this new double cutaway style resulted in a somewhat bulkier heel since the neck-to-body junction was maintained at the 16th fret.

The Melody Maker models were produced in very large quantities from the time of their introduction, and they remained tremendously popular until around 1967, when the figures began to dwindle. The series was eventually withdrawn in 1970, undoubtedly because the production costs had become too high for an "economy" model, which moreover had to face a fierce Japanese competition.

Even today after its discontinuation the Melody Maker remains a very good value for money on the second hand market, especially the examples manufactured between 1960 and 1962 as they provide a very nice, flat and wide, neck. In any case, it showed how an experienced company could produce a basic low priced instrument with craftmanship and care.

As regards solid body guitars, the 1950's were primarily a Les Paul period since the "other" models introduced by Gibson were — except for the Melody Maker — rather modest sellers. It is during the 1960's that the solid body guitar concept met with considerable success thanks especially to the "SG" series and to models like the EB-3 or the EB-O, not to mention the famous Firebird and Thunderbird guitars and basses.

Melody Maker "3/4" (1960)
Contrary to the three quarter size Les Paul Junior with a single cutaway, the neck-to-body junction was set at the $12^{th}$ fret and not at the $14^{th}$.

# CHAPTER 5

# THE EVOLUTION OF THE ELECTRIC ACOUSTIC GUITAR DURING THE 1950's THE FIRST "THIN LINE" MODELS

Gibson's entry in the field of "solid-body" guitars in 1952 was to pave the way for the development of a new breed of instrument, which, over the years received a greater attention and was eventually manufactured in quantities larger than ever. This was the result of both simpler methods of production and a change in the needs of guitar players in search of new sounds. For most of the fifties, however, the "traditional" electric acoustic guitar remained the flag-bearer of the company and as such it continued to progress and lead to the introduction of new models.

A little before the appearance of the first Les Paul model, Gibson unveiled the electric version of the Super 400 and the L-5, which in a way constituted the apex of the "amplified" guitar as opposed to a purely electric guitar (such as a solid body) with no acoustic property. Beginning in 1952 Gibson systematically altered its electric catalog, discontinuing or adding new models practically every year.

Thus in 1952, the decision was taken to stop the non-cutaway ES-300 and the different electric versions of the spruce top "L-7", namely, the L-7E, L-7ED, L-7CE and L-7CED. The last ES-300 guitars were shipped in 1953, while several L-7 electrics with Ted Mac Carty's fingerrest pick-ups were still delivered in 1954. Fingerrest pick-ups, however, continued to remain available until the 1960's in order to be adapted on the arch-top acoustic models of the Gibson line.

As a counterpart, Gibson introduced in 1952 a brand new model designated the **ES-295**, whose principal characteristic was to be entirely finished in the gleaming gold color used on the first Les Paul guitars. As a matter of fact, the prototype of the first-ever all gold guitar, which was merely a fancier ES-175 was conceived and exhibited to the public before the Les Paul model appeared

The ES-295 was for all purpose an ES-175 equipped with a second pick-up — in 1952, the ES-175 had only one — located near the bridge. As already mentioned it was painted gold and fitted with a Les Paul type trapeze bridge-tailpiece. By the way, the early 295's we happened to examine had the words "Les Paul" stamped on their tailpiece. The two pick-up assembly was completed by a volume and a tone control for each pick-up while preselection was made by means of a 3-position toggle switch.

Just like the ES-175 — as well as all the 16 1/4" body models of the Gibson range — the ES 295 had a fingerboard with only 19 frets and the neck-to-body junction was at the 14th fret. On the other hand, the pick-up cover and the fingerrest were made of a cream-colored plastic, and the pick-guard was even decorated with a gold floral design.

As for the designation it was in the

The ES-295 as it appeared in the 1952 catalog. Note the floral design on the pickguard.

On some of the early 295's the trapeze bridge-tailpiece did bear Les Paul markings.

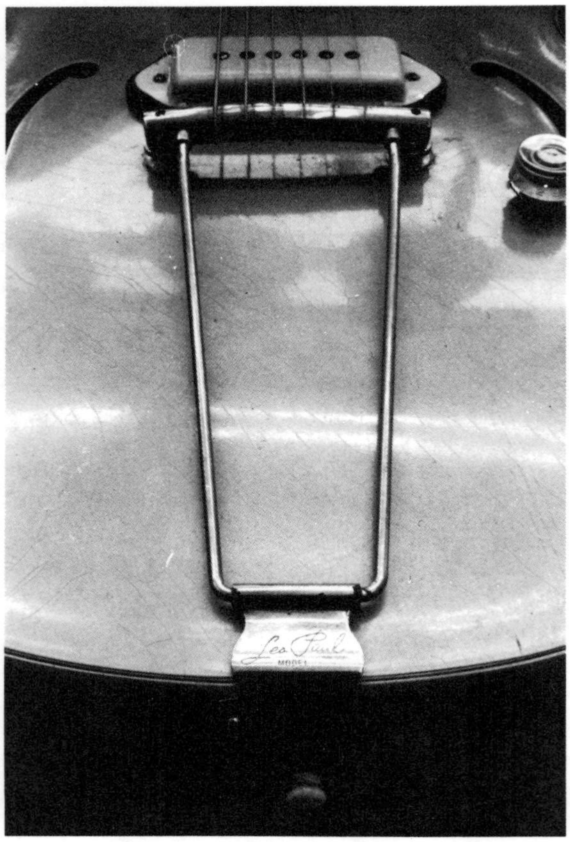

ES-175 D (1955) with two P-90's and a 20 fret fingerboard.

ES-175 (1953) fitted with an Alnico pick-up. The tailpiece of this example is not original.

ES-135 (1955) with "crown" position markers.

The J-160 E introduced in 1954.

ES-125 (1954) with pearl dot position markers.

A custom L-4 with two Alnico pick-ups and L-5 ornamentation.

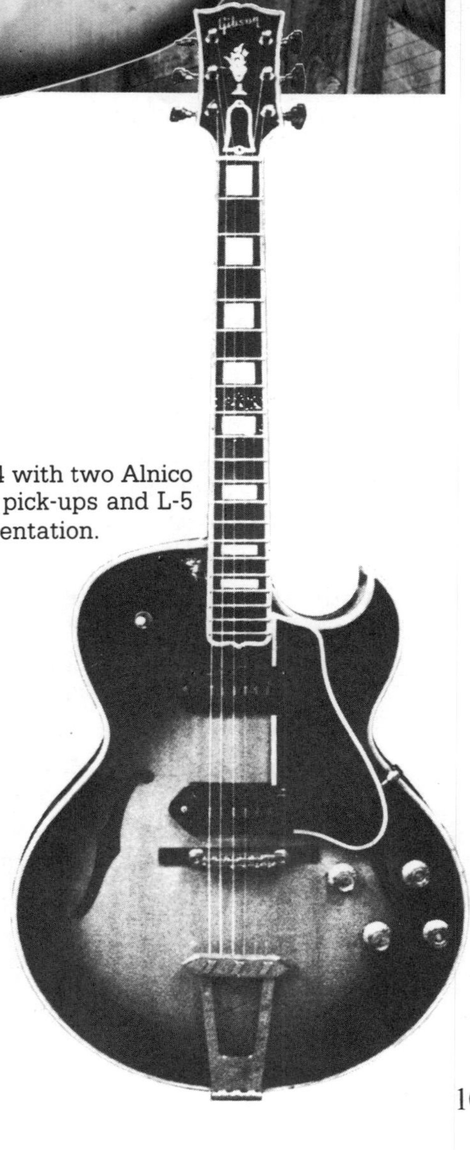

Gibson tradition related to the initial price of the instrument... $ 295.00 !

The 295 was to achieve a certain success with some of the young "Rock 'n' Roll" stars of the early 1950's before progressively falling into disuse as early as 1955 until its discontinuation in 1958. Scotty Moore recorded on the first "Sun" sessions of Elvis Presley with an ES-295 before switching over to an L-5 thanks to success.

Having equipped the ES-295 with two pick-ups, there was only one step to take for Gibson in order to fit the ES-175, introduced in 1949 as a single pick-up model, with a second unit. In 1953, a double pick-up version called the **ES-175D** appeared on the list dated July 1, 1953 at a price of $ 250.00 for the regular Sunburst model (ES-175D) and $ 265.00 for the "Natural" or "Blonde" variant (ES-175DN)... (this time, no connection between the price and the name !)

Around 1953 several ES-175's were fitted with an "Alnico" pick-up featuring direct adjustable magnets, instead of the usual P-90, probably in order to broaden the scope of the new pick-up. But these attempts did not prove too successfull as most people seemed to prefer the former type.

The following year, in 1954, an electric "Jumbo Flat Top" guitar made its appearance under the **J-160E** name. For Country and Western musicians it was basically a J-45 — with a body of 16 1/4" × 20 1/4" × 4 7/8" — that is a "Dreadnaught" acoustic model electrified by a small single coil pick-up installed at the end of the fingerboard. This pick-up was fitted with adjustable poles, and completed by volume and tone controls on top with a lateral out-put jack.

The J-160E had a laminated spruce top with mahogany back and rims while the bound fingerboard was made of rosewood with trapezoidal (or "crown") position markers. Like the 16 1/4" models of that time the fingerboard offered only 19 frets and the neck joined the body quite unusually at the fifteenth fret. The rosewood bridge was adjustable and like the other Gibson "Flat Top" guitars of this period it had a belly facing the fingerboard.

The J-160E complemented the CF-100E introduced earlier, and it enjoyed a much longer career since it was not discontinued until 1978. A few J-160E were factory made with a sharp cutaway on a custom order basis, and they look like bigger CF-100E. From the time of its introduction, several hundred J-160E guitars were produced each year, clearly evidencing the interest aroused by such an electric... John Lennon used his J-160E a lot in the early days of the Beatles.

Then Gibson waited until... 1955 to announce some change in the field of the "Electric Spanish" guitar, but these were not the least innovating decisions.

# THE ES-5 SWITCHMASTER

In 1955, Gibson offered an altered version of the 3 pick-up ES-5 under the name **"ES-5 Switchmaster"**.

Compared to the original model introduced in 1949, the new ES-5 Switchmaster was characterized by dual tone and volume controls for each pick-up... 6 knobs in all ! Then in order to remedy to the obvious inconvenience of the first ES-5 — i.e. the inability to switch immediately from one preset tone to another — Gibson equipped the guitar with a four way toggle switch placed on the upper bout, where the master tone control used to be. Of course these modifications gave to the new ES-5 a very unusual look whilst making it a really versatile electric guitar... quite certainly the world's most versatile guitar in 1955 !

The new toggle switch offered 4 preset positions, namely, any pick-up separately or all three simultaneously, but it was possible by turning down certain volume controls to obtain any two pick-up combination. Thus the ES-5 Switchmaster was offering unprecedented tonal possibilities.

Outside of this "electronic" alteration, the Switchmaster kept the same specifications as the regular ES-5 with a body entirely made of curly maple and a two piece maple neck with a dark wood seam. The rosewood fingerboard was ornamented with multiple black and white bindings and sported block pearl inlays.

The first examples of the new ES-5 were registered at the factory in July 1955 (serial numbers A 21063 and on) and the ES-5

A favorite among discriminating artists who demand impressive appearance, versatility and outstanding response. The ES-5 Switchmaster introduces many new and exclusive features emphasizing an increased range of performance, the latest electronic advances and real "playability."

Arched top and back of highly figured, curly maple with matching curly maple rims • alternate black and white ivoroid binding • modern cutaway design • three-piece curly maple neck with Gibson Adjustable Truss Rod • bound rosewood fingerboard with block pearl inlays • Tune-O-Matic bridge three powerful, humbucking pick-ups with individually adjustable pole pieces • separate tone and volume controls which can be preset • four-way toggle switch to activate each of the three pick-ups separately, in combination of any two, or all three simultaneously • gold-plated metal parts • exclusive new tailpiece design • laminated pickguard with attractive border individual machine heads with deluxe buttons.

SPECIFICATIONS

17" wide, 21" long, 3⅜" deep, 25½" scale, 20 frets

| | |
|---|---|
| **ES-5N**—Natural Finish | **$475.00** |
| **ES-5**—Sunburst Finish | **450.00** |
| **No. 600 Case**—Faultless, plush lined | **52.50** |
| **No. 606 Case**—Faultless, flannel lined | **42.50** |
| **No. ZC-6 Zipper Case Cover** | **30.00** |

Excerpt from the 1958 catalog depicting the ES-5 Switchmaster. Note the discrepancy between the text which mentions Humbucking pick-ups and the illustration which shows P-90's.

Carl PERKINS and his Switchmaster

Reproduction of the Switchmaster electric circuitry supplied by the Gibson factory.

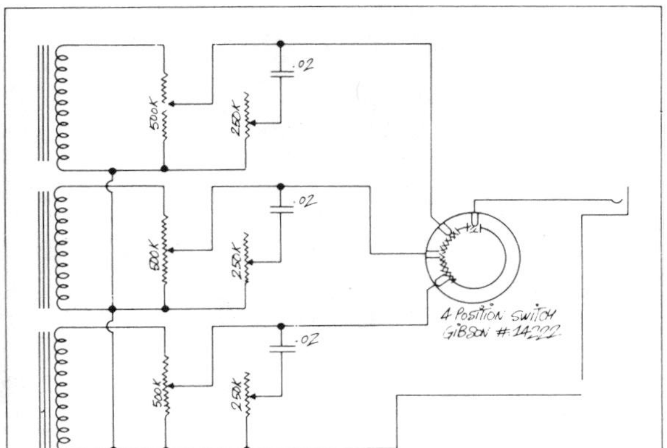

The concept behind the "Thin line" models is clearly illustrated
by this view of an ES-225 T next to an ES-175 D...
the difference in the body depth is quite obvious.

ES-225 T (1955)
Note the position of the pick-up,
half-way between the bridge
and the fingerboard.

ES-225 TDN (1957)

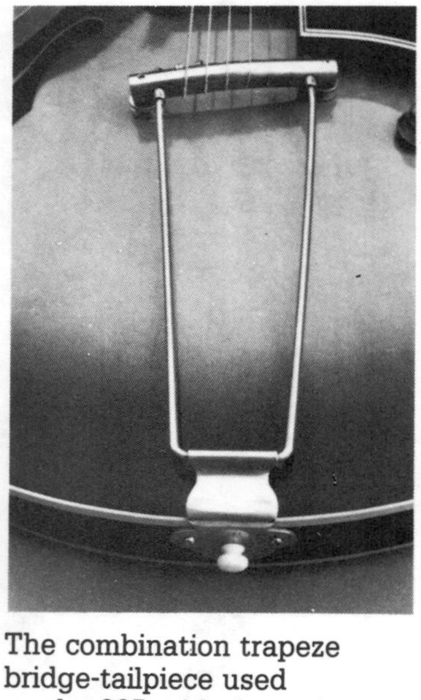

The combination trapeze
bridge-tailpiece used
on the 225 with the strings
passing "above"
the cylindrical bar and not
"under" as on the early
Les Paul models.

Switchmaster was featured on the September 15, 1955 list at a price of $ 450.00 for the "Sunburst" model and $ 475.00 for the "Natural" (or Blonde) edition.

Despite its phenomenal characteristics, the "Switchmaster" was considerably less expensive than the SUPER 400 CES which sold then for $ 675.00 in Blonde finish.

The first Switchmasters were still equipped with a classic trapeze tailpiece with a pointed string retainer, then starting in 1956 a fancier tailpiece with two elongated loops (remotely looking like "88") was adopted with the name ES-5 engraved on the upper part.

Later on the ES-5 was equipped with the new Humbucking pick-ups around the end of 1957. Then for its last year of existence it was modified at the end of 1960 to receive — like the L-5 CES, the SUPER 400 CES or the Byrdland — a sharp Florentine cutaway instead of the original rounded Venitian cutaway. The last ES-5 guitars were shipped in 1961 and the model was withdrawn from the 1962 catalog (printed in early 1961).

As for the original, non-Switchmaster ES-5 a few were still shipped in 1956 due to the casual overlap between two models, when one is introduced and the other is discontinued.

The ES-5 Switchmaster is a very unusual guitar among the Gibson line because of its unique electronic wiring. However, it was not to prove a decisive sales argument, since most players didn't care all that much about its electronic gimmickery rejected by both Jazzers and Rockers. The Switchmaster was doomed although someone like Carl Perkins made good use of this unordinary instrument.

In 1955, Gibson stopped the production of the 17" wide ES-150 and replaced it with the **ES-135.** The ES-135 was, in fact, a more richly decorated version of the ES-125 (dimensions of 16 1/4" × 20 1/4") whose top and bottom were made of maple, while the rims and the neck were of mahogany. The very first ES-135 appeared in 1954, but the real production did not start until 1955. Compared to the 125, the 135 stands out especially because of its bound fingerboard with trapezoidal position markers, and by its fingerrest made of several layers in black and white. The ES-135 was however manufactured in fairly small quantities for a model of this type and it was discontinued as early as 1958. Gibson had certainly realized that the one pick-up solid body guitars were selling faster and in any case the ES-125 was still there as a low budget one pick-up hollow body... hence exit the 135 !

As for the ES-150, which was from 1945 a 17" body model, the very last ones were shipped in 1956. Curiously, neither the ES-135 nor the ES-150 appeared in the 1956 Gibson catalog. This goes to show that certain catalogs are misleading either concerning the specifications or as regards the availability of a model. Nevertheless, the ES-150 still appeared in the September 15, 1955 list at the price of $ 190.00, while the ES-135 retailed at only $ 175, in July 15, 1957 and the ES-125 at $ 145.

# THE FIRST THIN LINE MODELS

1955 was, however, more than anything the year when Gibson introduced the all new "**Thin Line**" models which are not to be confused with the ES-335 style "semi-acoustic" or "semi-solid" models that we will examine in the next chapter. The thin line guitars are originally acoustic, but as their name implies, the depth of the body has been reduced to around half the size of the traditional acoustic models, hence a "thin body".

With the great development of the electric guitar since the early 1950's Gibson realized that the "big" hollow body guitars or even the new "solid body" models were not sufficient to satisfy the changing needs of the new generations of electric guitarists.

This relative inadequacy of the available equipment with the musical currents of the time promptly received a response from Gibson, with, starting in 1955, the "Thin-Line" and then in 1958 the "Semi-Solid" models.

Gibson's objective was obviously to offer an alternative to the guitarist who did not see the instrument that suited him in a guitar with a 3 3/8" deep body or in a relatively heavy solid body.

Consequently the **ES-225T** appeared in 1955, soon followed by the first Byrdlands and ES-350T's.

The 225T (T stands for Thin Line) took on the dimensions of 16 1/4" × 20 1/4" and the sharp Florentine cutaway of the ES-175, but differed because of a Les Paul type combination bridge-tailpiece (identical to the one on the ES-295) and naturally its reduced body thickness of 1 5/8" (1 3/4" in the 1958 and 1959 catalogs) compared to 3 3/8" for the 175 or the 295.

The top, back and rims were laminated maple, while the one piece mahogany neck had a bound rosewood fingerboard with pearl dot markers. From its introduction in 1955, the 225T was fitted with a 20 fret fingerboard as opposed to 19 for the different 16 1/4" wide guitars of that time. In fact, starting in 1955, these 16 1/4" models — i.e. ES-175, ES-175D, ES-295, ES-125, ES-135 and even J-160E — were also given a 20 fret fingerboard, while all the 17" wide models always had (with the exception of the ES-250) a 20 fret fingerboard.

On the 225T, the Gibson logo was pearl inlaid but the headstock did not carry the crown design found on the 175 or the 295.

The pick-up was of the usual single coil type (P-90) with surface covers. It was not placed at the end of the fingerboard or near the bridge, but **halfway** between the fingerboard and the bridge, so as to obtain, undoubtedly, a "different" sound.

The reduced body depth and the placement of the pick-up clearly showed Gibson's concern to offer an instrument with an "intermediate" tonal capacity.

In 1955, only the 225T (with one pick-up) was available at the price of $ 179.50 in a Sunburst finish. Starting in 1956, however, a two pick-up version called the **ES-225TD** was offered with a choice for the 225T and the 225TD between a "Sunburst" and a "Natural" finish.

The ES-225TD was naturally fitted with the usual Gibson wiring including dual volume and tone controls for each pick-up, plus a three way toggle-switch located in the upper bout.

In July 15, 1957, the 225 range retailed as follows :

| | | |
|---|---|---|
| ES-225T | (Sunburst) | $ 189.50 |
| ES-225TN | (Natural) | $ 204.50 |
| ES-225TD | (Sunburst) | $ 229.50 |
| ES-225TDN | (Natural) | $ 244.50 |

These four models were manufactured until 1959, then considering the impracticality of the Les Paul combination bridge-tailpiece, they were superseded by the ES-125TC and TCD models whose specifications are practically indentical, but for the bridge tailpiece section and the finish. During its rather short life's span, the 225 did sell fairly well as nearly 8000 of them were manufactured, although it was never a first rank instrument played by top names. However, some will recall Niki Sullivan played one while he was with Buddy Holly and the Crickets.

# THE BYRDLAND AND THE ES-350 T

The Byrdland and the ES-350T guitars were announced simultaneously in mid-1955 to consolidate the new "Thin Line" style launched by the company. Both took on — with the exception of the depth — the advanced format of 17" × 21" (like an L-5 or an ES-350) but were characterized by a 2 1/4" thick body compared to the 3 3/8" of all the other acoustic models of that time (the 225T excluded, naturally).

The **Byrdland** designation came from the contraction of the names of two guitarists, Billy **BYRD** and Hank Gar**LAND.**

At that time Billy Byrd was a well known guitarist in country music, and he became famous more particularly with Ernest Tubb (and his Texas Troubadours) who played regularly at the Grand Ole Opry in Nashville. Hank Garland was also considered mainly as a country guitarist, but he soon appeared equally as an excellent jazz guitarist whose career, which had a bright future was brutally interrupted in the early 1960's by a car accident that left him an invalid for a long time.

It is hard to assess which part Billy Byrd and Hank Garland took exactly in the

BYRDLAND (1957)

A close-up view of the Alnico pick-ups used on the Byrdland. Note the marble-like fingerrest.

Billy BYRD

The Byrdland headstock with the flower-pot or torch inlay already found on the L-5.

conception of the Byrdland. In fact, it is nearly certain that they had — like most artists who have an instrument named after themselves no actual participation in the final design of the guitar. Nevertheless, it is very likely that they "suggested" the idea of a "thinner" guitar with a "shorter" neck. Gibson pays a lot of attention to the remarks of guitarists, and particularly to great professionals, and consequently, it is plausible that the idea of the Byrdland was sparked off by them asking Gibson for a somewhat thinner "L-5" with a special neck. As a matter of fact a number of photos of Billy Byrd or Hank Garland, show them playing what is visibly and structurally a "Byrdland" but equipped with an "L-5" style tailpiece. These guitars could be early prototypes of the series or simply custom made guitars. Anyway, the Byrdland was launched as the fruit of the requirements of these two famous Nashville-based guitarists who in exchange for their adhesion received a royalty from Gibson.

When the new model was introduced the Birdland of New York (with an "i") tried, according to Ted MacCarty, to prevent Gibson from using this name, but failed because of the origin of the name (a contraction) and the spelling (the "y").

The Byrdland took on the structure and the materials used on the L-5 CES, that is, a solid spruce top, with flamed maple back and rims as well as a laminated curly maple neck with an ebony fingerboard and pearl block markers. The famous "flower pot" inlay already found on the L-5 was also transferred to the Byrdland.

However a new three-loop tailpiece with the "Byrdland" name engraved on the upper bar was used instead of the silver and gold unit in order to distinguish the new guitar from the aforementioned. Otherwise Kluson "sealfast" tuning gears were installed as on the L-5 CES. Lastly the Byrdland was initially given the same pearloid pickguard with a "watered" effect as the Super 400's or the L-5's of the fifties. A darker tortoise shell fingerrest was fitted around the end of 1957 approximately when the pick-ups were changed for Humbuckers. As regards electronics, the Byrdland was equipped with two "Alnico" pick-ups with oblong adjustable magnets. To our knowledge, P-90 pick-ups were never used until the introduction of Humbuckers by the end of 1957. The usual Gibson wiring system with dual volume and tone controls plus a 3-position toggle switch and a lateral out-put jack completed the assembly.

The most salient features of the new Byrdland, besides the depth of the body were the characteristics of the neck. As a matter of fact, the Byrdland was originally conceived with a "short" neck, that is to say, a neck with a 23 1/2" scale length as opposed to 25 1/2" for an L-5 CES or 24 3/4" for an ES-175. With the exception of the "Three Quarter Size" models and their 22 3/4" scale length, the Byrdland really had a "shorter" neck than the rest of the electrics in the Gibson range. The purpose of such a short neck was to make easier the fingering of "twisted" chords whilst improving the playing speed.

Moreover the Byrdland (as well as the ES-350T) was fitted from the ouset with a 22 fret fingerboard, instead of 20 for an L-5 or an ES-175 (before 1955 the ES-175 only had a 19 fret fingerboard). The neck-to-body junction was still at the fourteenth fret but the Byrdland was then the only electric acoustic model to offer a 22 fret fingerboard which was otherwise a regular feature on the Les Paul (solid body) guitars. This accounts for the shorter space between the two pick-ups and allows to spot at first glance a Byrdland from an L-5 on a front view. This is more especially true when the original tailpiece has been removed and replaced by a Bigsby vibrato as it was frequently the case in the late fifties.

As for the restricted width at the nut there was a little more hesitation. The first prototypes had a narrow neck, then the Gibson R & D department changed his mind for fear to limit the impact of the new model, and enlarged the neck, only to revert shortly after to the original design, with a noticeably narrower neck.

On September 15, 1955, the Byrdland was offered in a golden Sunburst finish for $ 550.00, and in a gleaming Natural finish for $ 565.

**The ES-350T** model took on the overall characteristics of the Byrdland especially with respect to the body and neck dimen-

A blonde L-5 CT with Humbucking pick-ups. Commonly known as the George Gobel model, the L-5 CT is characterized by a thinner body than the regular L-5. It was usually offered in a gleaming red finish and this guitar is quite likely one of a kind.

The 3-loop Byrdland tailpiece.

BYRDLAND (1959) with Humbucking pick-ups.

ES-350 T (1958) with Humbucking pick-ups.

Chuck BERRY with the ES-350 T he used in the mid-fifties.

ES 140 T "3/4" (1958)

ES 125 T "3/4" (1958)

sions, but it differed in a number of details that were borrowed from the ES-350 (no "T") it was intended to replace in the Gibson line.

So, the body was entirely made of curly maple without a solid spruce top, and the bound fingerboard was of rosewood instead of ebony, with double parallelogram inlay. It lacked the black and white purfling of the Byrdland and the Kluson "sealfast" tuning gears which were replaced by regular keys with a tulip shaped plastic head. The tailpiece, though having a loop design vaguely resembling a "W" was different with the "ES-350T" name engraved in the upper part.

At the time of its introduction the 350T was equipped with 2 P-90 type single coil pick-ups, and not with the Alnico pick-ups found on the more expensive Byrdland. In other words the ES-350T was somewhat like a... less fancy Byrdland. According to the September 15, 1955 list price, it was available with a Sunburst finish at $ 395.00 whilst the "Natural" version cost $ 410.00.

The first ever Byrdland's and ES-350T's destined for the public were registered in 1955, more precisely with serial numbers A-20985/86/87 on June 30 , 1955 for the Byrdland and serial numbers A-21057 to A-21062 on July 11,1955 for the ES-350T. The two new models, however, were not delivered in quantity until 1956.

Although the original full body ES-350 was not listed by Gibson in September 1955, the very last models of this type were shipped in 1956 and so during that year, the 350 and 350T were both available.

To better outline the importance of these new models at the time of their introduction, let us recall that Chuck Berry, that giant of Rock promptly adopted the 350T — before changing later on in favor of the new semi-solid guitars — while Steve Cropper played a Byrdland in the early days of the Mar-Keys. Roy Clark is also famous for his long association with the Byrdland, which has enjoyed an undisputed popularity over the years, especially with rhythm and blues players.

Although the Byrdland and the ES-350T were not manufactured in large quantities owing to their price, the "Thin Line" models offered guitarists an additional choice and Gibson was not wrong in abundantly developing this new style of instrument starting in 1956.

# THE OTHER "THIN LINE" MODELS

As already mentioned the ES-225T was joined in 1956 by a double pick-up version designated the ES-225TD. Also in 1956, Gibson introduced a "T" version of the ES-125 on which the body depth was simply reduced from 3 3/8" to 1 3/4", while the other specifications remained the same. The first **ES-125T's** were shipped from the factory in 1956 but the model was not manufactured in quantities until 1957. On July 15, 1957 both the ES-125 and ES-125T retailed at $ 145. It is interesting to note, though, that very quickly the "thin line" version superseded the regular full depth model as regards the volume of sales, and in 1959 the ES-125T was definitely produced in larger quantities... a sign of times !

Again in 1956, a "thin line" version of the Three Quarter Size" ES-140 introduced in 1950, was made available with a 1 3/4" thick body which almost perfectly gave it the appearance of an acoustic Les Paul Junior. Unlike the ES-140, the **ES-140T** was offered from 1956 both in a "Sunburst" and a "Natural" finish, respectively at the price of $ 185 and $ 200

However, the latter (ES-140TN) was just available in small quantities until 1958, when only the sunburst model continued to be offered. The last examples of the full bodied ES-140 were, for their part, shipped throughout 1957. With the exception of the first 2 or 3 years of production, the ES-140T did not meet, however with the success of the other "thin line" guitars. Furthermore the shipping totals clearly show the ES-140T was manufactured in smaller quantities than the ES-140, athough it remained in the catalog for a longer period of time. Without a doubt the sixties heralded a wane in the popularity of the short neck "3/4" models.

In 1957, a double pick-up version of the ES-125T was commercialized under the designation **ES-125TD** at the price of $ 179.50

Louis STEWART playing a SUPER 400 CES

A late fifties L-5 CESN
with Humbucking pick-ups.

The Gibson galaxy of stars in the mid-fifties.

*"121" A 1956 ES-5 Switchmaster with its four-way toggle-switch in the upper cutaway bout.
Note the finely curled maple top of this instrument in the inserted photograph.*

*"122" — **Top left :** ES-175 D (1955) with two P-90's and a 20 fret fingerboard.
— **Bottom left :** ES-225 TD (1959).
— **Right :** The author with two gently faded ES-295's featuring the trapeze bridge-tailpiece perfected by LES PAUL. The "greener" guitar on the right was made in 1954 and the other 295 on the left in 1955. Unfortunately both instruments had lost their fancy scratch plate when this photo was shot.*

*"123" ES-175 D (1961) with Humbucking pick-ups. Note the fancier tailpiece adopted on the 175 around 1958.*

*"124" A 1957 Byrdland with Alnico pick-ups and an original Bigsby vibrato tailpiece fitted at the factory. Note the marble-like fingerrest.*

*"125" ES-350 T (1958) with Humbucking pick-ups.*

*"124/125" This 1959 Byrdland was factory equipped with a Varitone and a Bigsby vibrato. Note the difference in the material of the fingerrest compared to the 1957 Byrdland.*

*"126" ES-355 TD-SV (1959).
Introduced in late 1958 as the top model of the new semi-solid series, the 355 was (almost) systematically fitted with a vibrato tailpiece.
Note the black ring found around the Varitone switch on the first guitars equipped with this device.*

*"127" A 1959 "dot neck" ES-335.
Note the very rounded profile of the double cutaway — almost looking like Mickey Mouse ears ! — which is a characteristic feature of all the early semi-solid models.*

*"128" ES-345 TD (1960).
On this example the original tuning gears have been replaced with more recent machines.
— **Top left :** ES-330 TD (1960).
As typical of the early 330's, this instrument has pearl dot position markers and black plastic pick-up covers.*

Gibson

Gibson

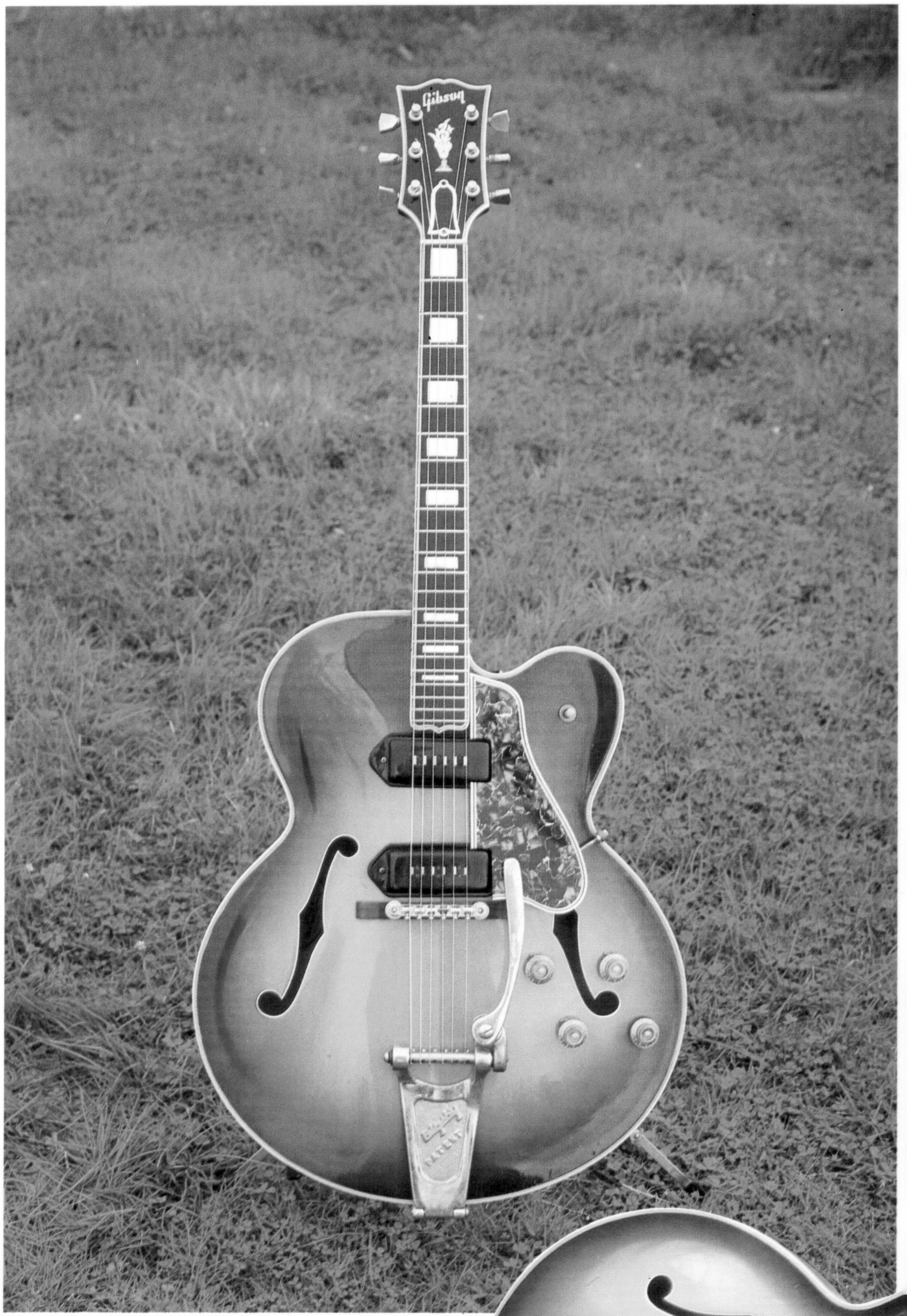

Gibson

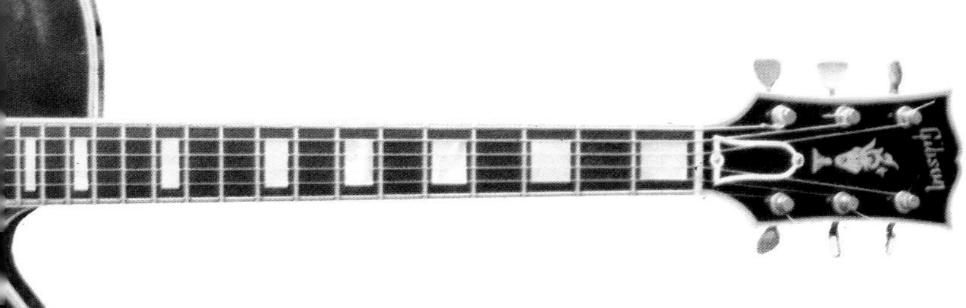

Gibson

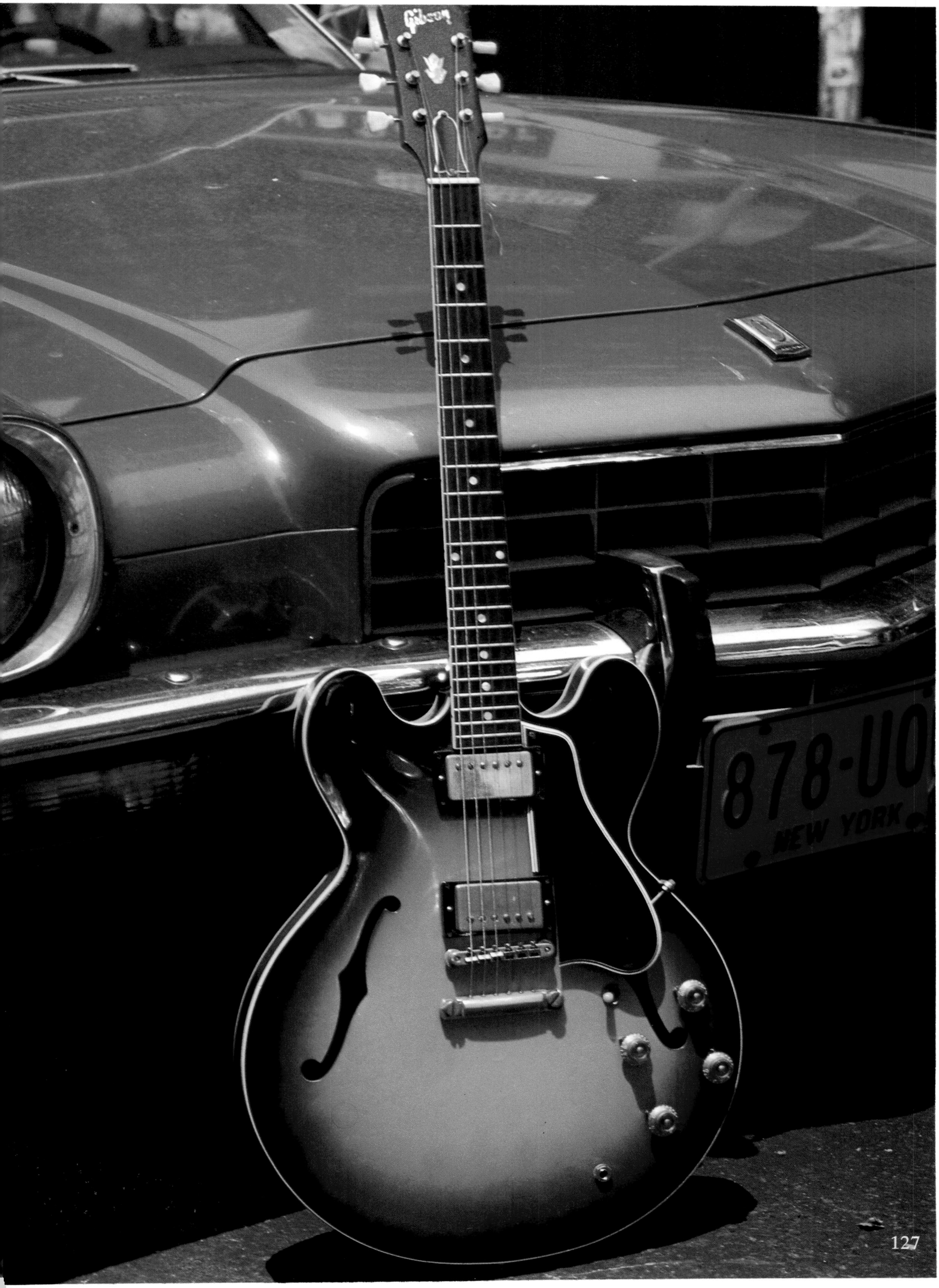
Gibson
878-UO
NEW YORK

Gibson
STEREO

compared to $ 145 for the one pick-up model. The ES-125TD was naturally fitted with dual volume and tone controls for each pick-up and a 3-way toggle switch. All the other specifications — dimensions or materials — were identical to the ES-125T.

The two pick-up model was manufactured in smaller quantities than the one pick-up, and the ES-125TD did not prove a big seller. Consequently it was stopped as early as 1963 after only 1200 units or so were produced in seven years. By comparison the sales of ES-125T reached frequently this figure (and above !) in a single year. A "three quarter size" variant of the ES-125T was also introduced in 1957 at the same price as the full size model ($ 145). It was manufactured until the late sixties in quantities similar to the ES-140T's. Contrary to the ES-140T, however, all the variants of the ES-125 introduced so far were instruments without a cutaway.

Starting around 1957 a growing number of guitars — especially the thin line models — were factory equipped with a "Bigsby" vibrato tailpiece which, moreover, had been shown as an accessory in the Gibson catalog since 1956. On July 15, 1957 the Bibsby unit cost $ 55 with regular plating ($ 66, with Tune-O-Matic bridge saddle) and $ 75 with gold plating ($ 90, with Tune-O-Matic). It is, therefore, not unusual to find Byrdlands or ES-350T's equipped from the outset with a Bigsby Vibrato, which was later even more systematically fitted to the various semi-solid models.

# THE END OF THE 1950's

As we have already seen in the chapter devoted to the Les Paul series, 1957 was the year when the Humbucking pick-up was officially introduced. Thus a growing number of models were progressively fitted with the new pick-up.

Between 1957 and 1958, the following electric spanish guitars had their single coil pick-ups (Alnico or P-90) replaced with Humbuckers : Super 400 CES, L-5 CES, Byrdland, ES-5 Switchmaster, ES-350T, ES-175D and ES-175. Naturally, until around the end of 1962, the pick-ups on these models exhibited a "Patent Applied For" label.

In 1958, Gibson took a new step in versatility by launching two double-neck models, respectively designated "**Double 12**" (6 and 12 strings) and "**Double Mandolin**" (6 strings and mandolin). The objective was simply to offer "two instruments in one" to the guitarist who had to play several parts in an orchestra or who, was looking for new sounds, thanks to the resonance between the 2 necks. Both models were structurally identical and had a spruce top with maple back and rims. The necks were one piece mahogany while the bound fingerboard was rosewood, with parallelogram position markers.

The double cutaway bodies of these instruments were hardly wider than a "normal" guitar, as with a 17 1/4" width, they were within the dimensions of a Super 400. The depth, was limited to 1 7/8" so that the two guitars were not too cumbersome or heavy. On the "Double 12", the lower neck was a regular guitar neck whereas the upper one had 12 strings. At the time, it was the first ever electric 12 string released by Gibson. Both necks had a scale length of 24 3/4" with 20 frets. Two Humbucking pick-ups with master volume and tone controls, were fitted to each neck with a 3-way toggle switch. A third toggle switch was used to select the neck to be played.

On the "Double Mandolin", the lower neck was also reserved for the guitar, while the much shorter upper neck — scale length 13 7/8" with 24 frets — belonged to a six-string mandolin. The electric assembly was identical to the "Double 12", except that the mandolin neck only had one Humbucking pick-up and thus the Double mandolin did not require 3 toggle-switches. Contrary to all the other necks (including the 12 string) the bridge for the mandolin was not a "Tune-O-Matic", but a rosewood saddle adjustable for height only.

The "Double 12" and "Double Mandolin" were, considering their unusual characteristics, custom built and available only on special order. Furthermore, the shipping totals indicate that these models were manufactured in rather modest quantities and are, as a consequence, very rare today. As to the finish, three options were offered in 1958 :

The first tailpiece used on the ES-175...

ES-175 DN (1960)

...and the fancier unit adopted around 1958.

Pat METHENY and his 175

ES-5 Switchmaster with Humbucking pick-ups. Note the new style tailpiece used by the end of 1956.

Double Twelve (1958)

A white 1960 Double 12. Note the raised spruce top typical of the early double-neck models.

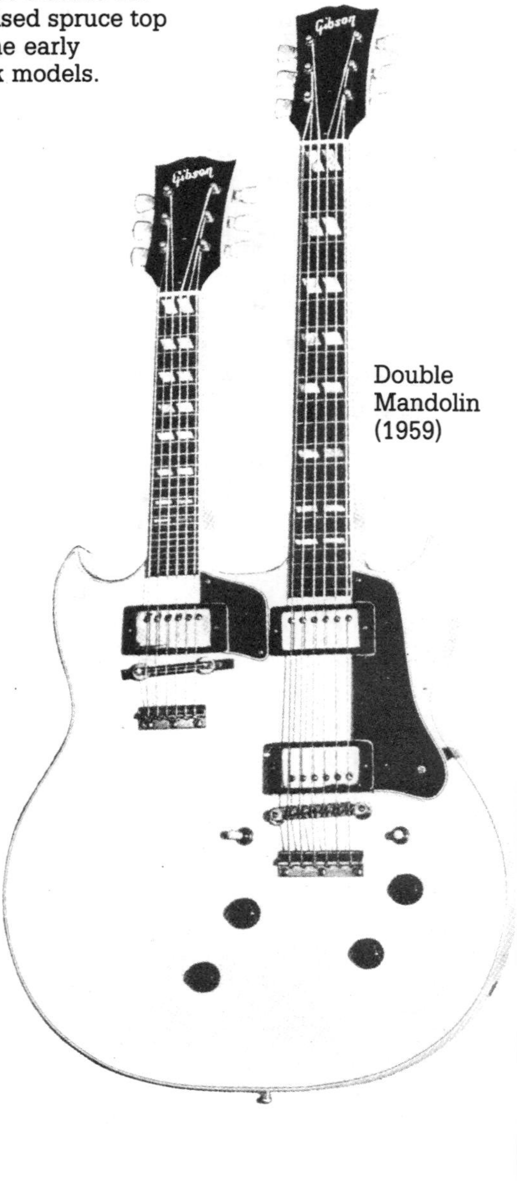

Double Mandolin (1959)

Sunburst, black and white. The "Double 12" cost $ 475.00 while the "Double Mandolin" went for $ 435.00.

The "Double Neck" models kept this shape and structure with a raised top until 1962, when they took on a new solid body design clearly inspired from the "SG" style introduced in 1961.

In 1958, Gibson stopped the ES-295 whose entirely gold color, just like on the Les Paul, no longer appealed to guitarists, and the last ones were shipped during that same year. In 1959, the small CF-100E was dropped in turn as Gibson, no doubt, felt that the J-160E alone filled perfectly its role as an electric "Flat Top". At any rate the appearance of the J-160E in 1954 had markedly reduced the scope of the CF-100E, which was nevertheless manufactured in nearly 1300 examples during its 9 year life's span.

In 1958 and 1959, Gibson commercialized a batch (around 40 units) of a model designated **L-4 CE,** or in other words, an "electrified" L-4C which was originally a purely acoustic guitar. The L-4C was similar in shape to an ES-175, but it did have (unlike the 175) a solid "spruce" top. According to the Gibson registers, these L-4CE's were equipped with a "Charlie Christian" bar pick-up, which had been withdrawn from the factory electrics in 1940 but continued to be mounted "on special request" all through the 1940's, the 1950's and even the 1960's.

As a matter of fact the old bar pick-up always enjoyed some popularity among jazz players and this is the reason why it was still possible — by popular demand ! — to install this unit on a Gibson guitar. However, the specifications of the late fifties bar pick-up were somewhat different from the pre-war units as the coil was brought down from 10,000 to 8,700 turns of 42 wire. Hank Garland always had a bar pick-up in the front position on his personal Byrdland. As a further example of this popularity, Billy Byrd ordered in 1959 a L-5CT, which was fitted with two (!) bar pick-ups. The **L-5CT** was a "thin line" L-5 with a 2 3/8" deep body (instead of 3 3/8" for the standard L-5) and a shorter scale length of 24 3/4" (instead of 25 1/2"). It was expressly developed by Gibson for comedian George Gobel (hence the "George Gobel" nickname) who asked for the guitar to be finished in a gleaming cherry red. The **L-5CT** was manufactured from 1959 to 1961 in fairly small quantities (43 in all) but a few of them were factory equipped with humbuckers or bar pick-ups, although it was primarily introduced as an acoustic guitar next to the L-5C.

Likewise, it was also possible at this time to obtain from the Gibson factory a standard L-5 "equipped" with only one pick-up instead of two. Wes Montgomery, to mention only him, played for a long time on such a model. In fact, as already pointed out, it was then possible to order from Gibson a "custom" built guitar based upon an existing model. This policy lead to the appearance of "strange birds" such as a 175 made like an L-5 or a 125 with a Super 400 neck !

At the end of the 1950's, Gibson made available a special version of the one pick-up ES-125T, equipped with a 3-position toggle switch and dual volume and tone controls as if the guitar had actually two pick-ups and not one. The toggle switch allowed for a preselection of two electric circuits which had different capacitors. This wiring brought in interesting tonal combinations from only one pick-up but apparently it was never mentioned in a Gibson catalog. Thus the number of guitars with such a wiring system is presumably limited, if not scarce.

In 1960, Gibson decided to stop the 225 series and introduced a new model to replace it under a different designation, but for all practical purposes, with similar specifications. It was the **ES-125TC** (and **TCD**) which derived its name from an ES-125T fitted with a cutaway (C : Cutaway). Just like the ES-225 and the ES-125T, the ES-125TC had a 16 1/4" × 20 1/4" × 1 3/4" body with an ES-175 or ES-225 sharp Florentine cutaway. Compared to the latter, the 125TC was characterized by its "classic" trapeze tailpiece with a compensated rosewood saddle instead of the Les Paul type combination bridge-tailpiece. Like on the 125, the Gibson logo was applied with a gold decal and not pearl inlaid like on the 225.

Lastly the ES-125TC was offered in "Cherry Sunburst" (red-into-yellow) whereas the finish of the 225 was a much darker

ES 125 TC (1960)

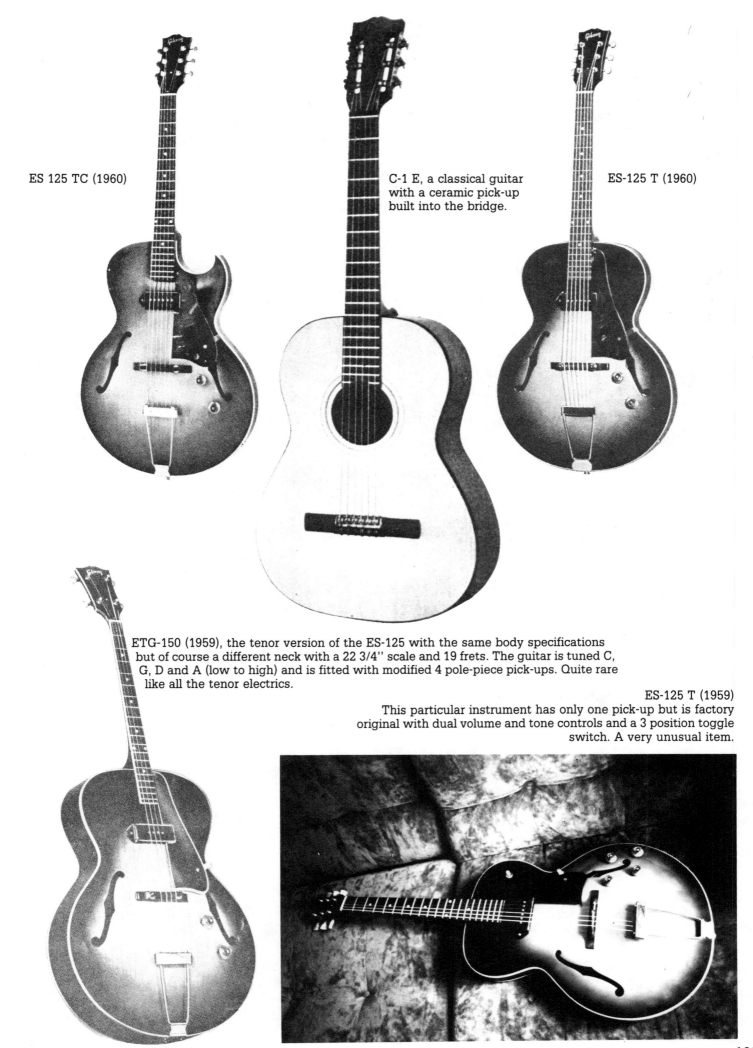

C-1 E, a classical guitar with a ceramic pick-up built into the bridge.

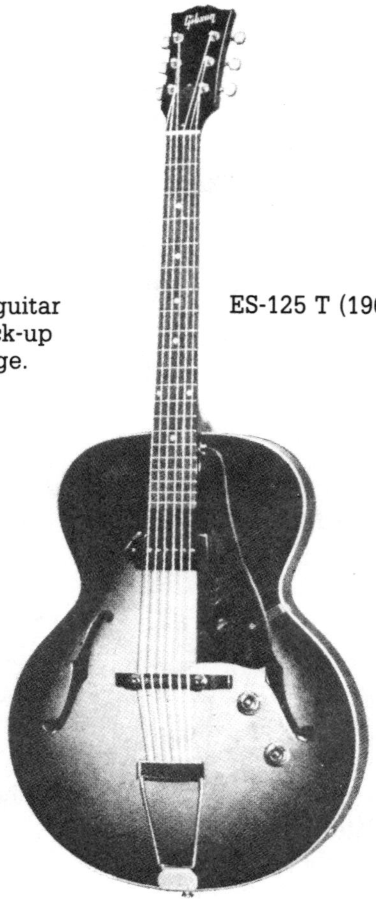

ES-125 T (1960)

ETG-150 (1959), the tenor version of the ES-125 with the same body specifications but of course a different neck with a 22 3/4'' scale and 19 frets. The guitar is tuned C, G, D and A (low to high) and is fitted with modified 4 pole-piece pick-ups. Quite rare like all the tenor electrics.

ES-125 T (1959)
This particular instrument has only one pick-up but is factory original with dual volume and tone controls and a 3 position toggle switch. A very unusual item.

sunburst (brown-into-yellow). The ES-125 was available, from 1960, in a single pick-up version (TC) at $ 185.00 and in a double pick-up version (TCD) at $ 225.00.

Fortunately, Gibson had stopped a few years ago using the price of a model to determine its designation !

Thanks to its cutaway the ES 125 TC quickly superseded the ES 125 T and all the other single coil thin-line models. In fact it was manufactured as early as 1960 in quantities exceeding one thousand units each year (ES 125 TC + ES 125 TCD).

On the threshold of the 1960's, Gibson ended a decade that witnessed an unprecedented evolution in the field of electric guitars, with the introduction of an electrified classical guitar called the "C 1-E". This model had the general characteristics of the C-1 classical guitar introduced earlier with a 14 1/4" × 19" × 4 1/2" body, a spruce top, mahogany back and sides. The neck was equally made of mahogany with a 19 fret rosewood fingerboard. As standard with classical guitar the scale was 25 1/2" long. The structure of the guitar as well as the neck width and shape were naturally in accordance with the existing norms for a classical guitar.

The ceramic pick-up placed in the bridge of the C 1-E was designed by Richard Evans, before he joined the Gibson staff as the full-time chief engineer of the Gibson electronics department in 1962. The C 1-E did not have a volume or tone control and except for a scrutinizing look at the bridge, only the lateral out-put jack established the fact that it was electric.

The C 1-E did not appear in the 1960 Gibson catalog published in May but it was nevertheless available in the latter part of the year, since the first examples of this rather unusual classical guitar were actually shipped in 1960. The model was featured for the first time in the 1962 catalog — dated May, 1961 — and it remained available until 1968.

The different electric models introduced by Gibson throughout the 1950's clearly emphasized the company's strong will to diversify its range and more especially to offer each guitarist the instrument that could best suit him. With this in mind, the appearance of the "Thin Line" models was, without a doubt a tremendous success, but Gibson was going to outdo itself by introducing in 1958, a radically new type of instrument combining various options formerly offered, such as the sound of a solid body guitar, but with a more acoustic feel. Although these new instruments were heralded under the "thin line" banner, we will refer to them as "semi-solid" guitars in order to clearly denote the difference in their structure.

Considering the importance of this series in the evolution of the electric guitar, the following chapter is entirely devoted to these new models which were introduced starting in 1958.

# CHAPTER 6

# A NEW TYPE OF INSTRUMENT... THE SEMI-SOLID GUITARS

The "Thin Line" series allowed Gibson to complete harmoniously its range of electrics between the traditional deep body electric acoustic models and the more recent solid body guitars. However, the "thin line" models were somehow more related to an acoustic instrument soundwise and "something else" had to be found to come closer to the tonal possibilities of a solid body.

Starting in 1957, Ted Mac Carty and his staff began to work on a new project in order to define what was to be a radically innovating type of instrument in structure as well as in shape. In fact, the objective was to create a guitar approaching, as nearly as possible, the sound of a solid body without its weight nor its peculiar feeling.

The Gibson R & D department imagined, at first, placing only a solid piece of wood on the inside of a guitar in the extension of the neck. The pick-ups and bridge could be mounted on this block... a little like Les Paul's "Log" in the 1940's. Owing to the weight and cumbersomeness, of such a block, Gibson chose to apply this idea to a "thin line" model, especially as the objective was to fill to gap between the "thin line" and the solid body guitars.

After finding the key principle for the structure of the instrument, a new design was brought about by the company with a rather classic inspiration since the guitar exhibited a curve on top and back and two "F" holes. In order to adapt to this curve, strips of spruce were glued to the body to allow the inner "chunk" of maple to be firmly attached inside the box.

A double rounded cutaway — totally original at the time — was created by Ted Mac Carty and his team, who discarded the traditional shapes like, say, a Byrdland or a 175 for the application of the new structure. This graceful form, both pretty and innovative at the same time with the dimensions of 16" × 19" × 1 3/4" allowed the neck to be cleared away from the body, making it easier to reach the treble end. Of course the center block of maple improved the sustain, while separating the body into two distinct acoustic cavities, each one with an "F" hole. Thus, the guitar had a certain acoustic resonance while carefully avoiding the eventual feed-back problems that can arise on an electric acoustic model.

The result could be qualified as "Semi-Solid" or "Semi-Acoustic" depending on the point of view and as far as we are concerned we will retain the first name which better described the objective sought-after by Gibson who had succeeded in finding the intermediate instrument which perfectly completed its line. Now the only thing left was to promote it !

The first semi-solid models were announced in the February 1958 issue of the "Gibson Gazette". They were a guitar designated ES-335 T and a 4-string bass, which being the second electric bass in the history of Gibson, was simply called the EB-2 (Electric Bass No. 2).

## THE ES-335 T

The **ES-335 T** model is characterized, like all the models of the series, by a body entirely made of maple with a center block also of maple, glued to several spruce strips in order to fit the arch of the top and of the back. Considering its structure, a solid spruce top would not have been justified and laminated maple was used throughout.

The neck consisted of a single piece of mahogany with a rosewood fingerboard which remained without any binding until approximately the end of 1958 as we came across several guitars of that period with unbound fingerboards (e.g. ES-335 with a number A 28415).

The fingerboard had 22 frets with pearl dot position markers in the usual places, hence the current nicknames of the early 335's such as "dot inlay" or "dot marker". The scale length was the usual 24 3/4" and the junction of the neck to the body took place — a particularly interesting characteristic — at the 19th fret, and not at the 20th as indicated in the first catalogs.

As regards the shape of the neck itself, the first 335 of 1958 had a nice clubby neck with a round profile. Then starting in 1960 it became flatter and wider, like on the Les Paul Standard of the same period. It remained this way until approximately 1963 when it kept more wood in the upper registers with a slightly narrower neck. For exemple a 335 made in 1961 has a width close to 43 mm at the nut whilst the neck is only a mere 22 mm thick at the 12th fret. Otherwise the Gibson logo, as well as the classic "crown" design were inlaid on the peghead.

From the time of its introduction, the 335 was fitted with two Humbucking pick-ups which, naturally, until around the end of 1962, showed a "Patent Applied For" label. Separate volume and tone controls for each pick-up, plus a 3-position toggle switch completed the assembly, while the out-put jack was located on top of the guitar near the controls.

Initially the ES-335 was released with a stop-tailpiece — identical to the one used on the Les Paul guitars — and a Tune-O-Matic bridge. However, a large number of 335's were factory equipped in the late 1950's, with a "Bigsby" vibrato tailpiece, and in this case, a small plate reading "Custom Made" was nailed (or glued) behind the bridge, in order to conceal the holes intended for the stop tailpiece.

As for "characteristic details", besides the fingerboard with its pearl dot inlay, the first ES-335 T's are distinguishable by a longer scratch-plate extending beyond the "Tune-O-Matic" bridge and hiding half of the lower "F" hole. Also, on the first edition there is a rather deep adjustment of the neck with the body as well as much slenderer "F" holes. Lastly, on all the early models of the semi-solid series, the very rounded design of the double cutaway (... almost like Mickey Mouse ears) must be noted as a slightly more "pointed" profile, was adopted starting in 1963. In fact, it looks as though the body underwent minor changes in the early sixties' since, besides the shape of the cutaway, the first semi-solids appear to be somewhat "thinner" at the rim by a fraction of an inch, than the subsequent models.

The new ES-335 was first shown in the "Gibson Gazette" of February 1958, but it also appeared on the last page of the March 25, 1958 catalog next to the Flying V.

According to the Gibson ledgers, the first production ES-335's were recorded on April 21, 1958 (serial numbers A 27483, 484, 485, 486) and as early as 1958, a very large number of 335 T's and TN's were commercialized, clearly indicating the interest immediately raised by this new class of instrument.

It is highly probable though that the first 335's (and EB-2's) were actually begun in the latter part of 1957, after Gibson had completed its prototypes during the same year.

The 335 "T" took on a "TD" designation starting in 1960 while the "long" pickguard was not replaced by a shorter one, stopping abreast of the lead pick-up, until the very beginning of 1961.

The pearl dot position markers were superseded by small rectangular "block" inlays in the course of 1962. However the very first 335's of 1962 with "block inlay" — as opposed to "dot inlay" — were still equipped with "P.A.F." pick-ups. Then Gibson started using "P.A.F." and "Patent Number" pick-ups randomly on its guitars until the beginning of 1963 when all the Humbuckers were definitely labeled with the Patent Number (N° 2737842). Later on, the stop-tailpiece was equally replaced by a

ES-335 T (1958)
This guitar bearing serial number A-27914 is one of the very early 335's for besides its pearl dot position markers it has an unbound fingerboard.

Larry CARLTON : Mr 335

ES-335 TD (1960)

This close-up view clearly shows the "long" pickguard extending beyond the Tune-O-Matic bridge, as well as the "Custom Made" plaque located over the stop-holes on the models fitted with a vibrato tailpiece.

One of the rare 335's factory equipped with a Varitone.

A custom hybrid model... this is not a 345 without a Varitone but a 1959 ES 335 fitted with a 345 fingerboard (note the single binding on the body). Unfortunately this guitar has lost its long scratchplate.

A beautiful flame maple top ES-335 TN from 1959.

Dave EDMUNDS "Rockpiling" with a dot neck 335

traditional Gibson trapeze tailpiece around the end of 1964.

The finishes offered in Spring of 1958 were the usual "Sunburst" and "Natural" shades priced respectively at $ 267.50 (ES-335 T) and $ 282.50 (ES-335 TN). Some rare 335's were finished in red, probably on a special order basis, in late 1958 (they were, however, not listed separately by Gibson).

The stock "Cherry Red" color, though, was not officially adopted for the 335 until 1960 under the designation ES-335 TDC. This "Red" finish was meant actually to replace the "Natural" finish discontinued in 1960, after a relatively small number of 335's had been offered with this option (209 to be exact). Later on "Cherry Red" was to become throughout the 1960's the main finish of the 335 to the detriment of the original "Sunburst".

As regards serial numbers, the 335, like all the models of the semi-solid series, was until February 1961 supplied with a number preceded by the letter "A" (ex. A 31913) written on an orange oval label directly underneath the upper "F" hole. From around February 1961 it had a 4, then 5, then 6 digit number written as before, on an orange oval label but also imprinted in the wood on the back of the headstock.

For more complete details, it is recommended to refer to the appendix dealing with identification numbers, but the important thing to remember is that a model having a number stamped in the wood behind the headstock would not have been shipped from the factory before 1961.

# THE EB-2 BASS

The **EB-2** bass, outside the new double cutaway form, took on a certain specifications of the EB-1 ("violin") bass introduced in 1953, such as a 30 1/2" scale length with 20 frets, a one-piece bridge tailpiece, vertical banjo-like Kluson tuning machines and above all the famous (25,000-turns or so !) bass pick-up. Naturally, because of its form and structure the EB-2 was, however, a totally different instrument from the EB-1.

Like the 335, it had an entirely maple body with a one piece mahogany neck and an unbound rosewood fingerboard. The neck joined the body at the eighteenth fret in order to clear the upper registers (up to E-Flat), as the new bass was meant to offer the same unprecedented advantages as the guitar. The Gibson logo was inlaid in pearl on the headstock as well as the classic crown design.

The first EB-2's were equipped with only volume and tone controls, then beginning in 1959, a Bass/Baritone switch was added to give the EB-2 a broader tone register. On the first EB-2's the pick-up cover was of brown bakelite with the poles located on the bottom edge of the pick-up, opposite to the bridge like on the EB-1. Around 1960, the poles were moved to the center of the pick-up and later on, the bakelite cover was replaced by a metal one, while a damper was fitted to the bridge.

Also at the end of 1960, the vertical tuning machines were replaced by Klusons with perpendicular keys. The first type of tuning machines is quite remarkable as on a front-view photo, it looks as though the bass has no keys at all !

Options identical to those of the 335 were offered in 1958 for the finish, namely "Sunburst" at the price of $ 267.50 and "Natural" at $ 282.50. However a few EB-2's were shipped in Black around May 1959, and in Red around March 1960, but officially the EB-2 was only available in the two traditional finishes.

The EB-2 was not shown in the 1962 Gibson catalog (dated May 1961) as it was temporarily discontinued. The last models of the first period were shipped in 1961 with a Sunburst finish as the Natural model was only offered until 1960. The EB-2 bass was not manufactured in 1962 or 1963, and the model did not reappear until 1964 (with a sunburst finish only).

Later on, a double pick-up version was introduced as the EB-2 D.

# THE ES-355 T

After the introduction of the 335 and the EB-2, Gibson completed its line of semi-solid guitars by offering other models based

# Gibson thin-body guitars feel just right

Whenever guitar players get to talking about their favorite instrument there's one thing they'll always say: *the feel is right!* And that's just what they've all been saying about Gibson's great new series of thin-body electrics. Yes, every one of these models—each with the Gibson *wonder-thin silhouette*—really does have that certain "feel" to it. And fitting so close and comfortably to your body, it'll let you reach many chords easily you've never played before.* You'll find the slender Gibson neck feels just right in your hand, and it's so easy to finger. That extremely fast, low action will make the strings seem feather-light to your touch. If you haven't done so already, be sure to find out all about this new all-star line of light-weight low-action thin-body Gibsons . . . each model so easy to handle, so easy to play. All have that quick response, balanced tone that always says instantly—Gibson.

Gibson INC.

KALAMAZOO, MICHIGAN

**the Gibson wonder-thin silhouette . . .** *only 1¾" to 2¼" thin . . . in a full series of Gibson guitars, priced from $145 to $605.*

* *Especially with Gibson's beautiful, cherry-red ES-355T double cutaway model, you'll reach right down to the very last fret with the greatest of ease (shown here, along with the GA-400 amp, by Gibson artist-enthusiast, Andy Nelson).*

A late fifties ad introducing the "thin line" models and more especially the semi-solid guitars. In this picture Andy Nelson is playing a Mono 355 fitted with a Custom L-5 neck.

EB-6 (1960) with bass baritone push button switch.

EB-2 (1960)

Close up view of the second version of the EB-2 pick-up with the pole pieces now moved in the middle of the cover.

The Kluson tuning gears used on the early EB-2's

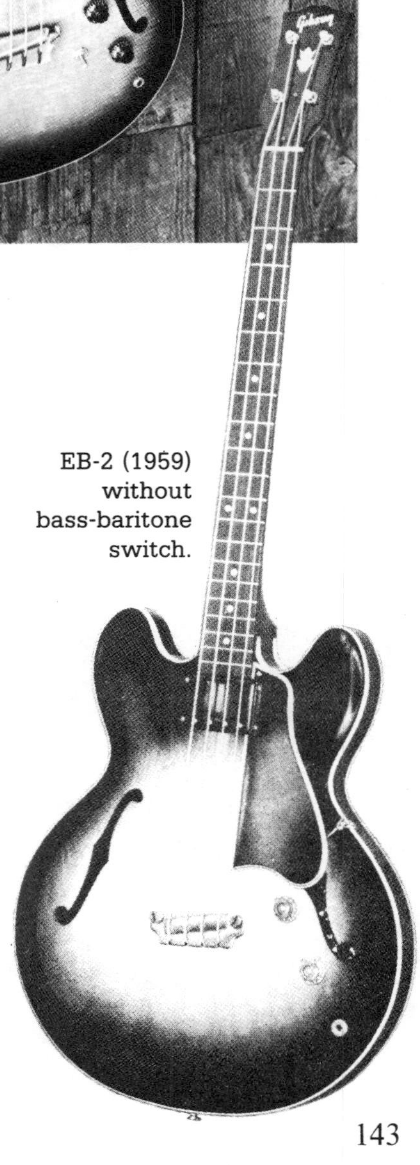

EB-2 (1959) without bass-baritone switch.

# "IN THE GIBSON GALAXY OF STARS..."

*"145" The late WES MONTGOMERY with a one pick-up L5-CES.*

*"146" One of the fathers of Rock'n'Roll... Chuck BERRY in a humoristic mood with an ES-355.*

*"147" Joe PASS demonstrating his virtuoso lines with an ES-175 D.*

*"148" AL DI MEOLA... or how to play Fusion music on a vintage LES PAUL Standard.*

*"149" Among the great Rock-guitar heroes of all time... Jeff BECK and his modified LES PAUL Standard.*

*"150" One of the most influential stylists of the last decade, John MAC LAUGHLIN in concert with an ES-345.*

*"151" Steve HOWE of YES-Fame with his dearly beloved ES-175 D.*

*"152" BLUES ~~BOY~~ MASTER KING with one of his Lucilles.*

on the same concept but with variations in the finish or in the electronics.

The first model of this second wave was a fancier version of the ES-335 called the **ES-355.** It was officially announced in the March-April 1959 issue of the "Gibson Gazette", but according to the Gibson ledgers, the first ones were registered in November 1958 (serial numbers : A 28413 and on), and thus a few of them were actually shipped by the end of that year.

The 355 is characterized by an ebony fingerboard (instead of rosewood) slightly narrower than the 335 with rectangular pearl block inlays. According to Gibson's introduction text the one piece neck was made of Peruvian mahogany ! The headstock had the split diamond design found on the Super 400 or the Les Paul Custom, as well as multiple black and white bindings. The same bindings were found on the upper edge of the body while the lower edge was less richly decorated. The metal parts were naturally gold-plated and the 355 was factory equipped with the then new Grover Rotomatic tuning machines, whereas the 335 had only regular tulip-shaped Kluson tuners. Though narrower, the neck of the 355 followed the evolution of the 335 as regards its thickness and profile.

In comparison with the 335, the 355 was, from 1958 on, practically always equipped with a vibrato-tailpiece which on the very first models was systematically a Bigsby unit. It is possible though, that a few samples were originally assembled with a stop-tailpiece but they are, to our knowledge very rare. If in doubt, one only needs to look at the base of the guitar for the traces of the screws used to mount the vibrato.

The 355 like the 335 was fitted with two Humbucking pick-ups with independant volume and tone controls for each pick-up, plus the usual 3-position toggle switch. The scratch-plate had additional bindings but kept the long format introduced on the 335.

The first version of the 355 introduced in 1958 was a "monophonic" model (as opposed to stereophonic) without the Varitone system introduced only in 1959. It was in theory available only with a "Cherry" finish at the price of $ 495.00. However, a few samples were also made in black, and even in white, between 1958 and 1960, probably by special order.

In 1959 a second version was introduced under the designation **ES-355 TD-SV** (S : Stereo, V : Varitone). Unlike the preceding model, the 355 TD-SV was not only mounted in Stereo (with the words engraved on the truss rod cover) but it also has a six position tone control known as a Varitone.

This "Varitone" rotary switch, consists in a series of capacitors of different values which progressively "dry" out the sound of the pick-ups by filtering certain frequencies. The Varitone system was invented by Walter Fuller and it is a very ingenious "passive" device that, combined with the two pick-ups, allows the guitarist to obtain 18 basic sounds. A certain number of 335's were also equipped with this system on a special order basis as well as some Byrdlands (see color photo).

On all the first semi-solid models fitted with a Varitone (ES-355 and ES-345), the ring indicating the six positions was black, then it was permanently changed to gold.

Starting in 1960, the number of ES-355 produced in stereo with a Varitone became much greater than those in mono, but both models, were manufactured simultaneously until 1970 when the mono version was eventually dropped.

In the course of 1960, the regular Bigsby vibrato was somewhat superseded by a new "sideways" vibrola perfected by Gibson. Unlike the Bigsby, on which the player had to push vertically "against" the strings to obtain the effect, the new vibrato had to be pulled in a motion perpendicular to the strings to get the same results. Later on in 1963, the Sideways Vibrola which was equally featured on the new Les Paul/SG introduced in 1961 was dropped in favor of a much simpler unit with a vertical action. This new vibrola is recognizable thanks to its metal cover engraved with a lyre and the Gibson logo and is often called "Maestro Vibrola". It was, however, still possible during this period to order a semi-solid guitar which was factory equipped with a Bigsby vibrato, and not with the "Sideways" unit or the "Maestro Vibrola".

ES-355 TD-SV (1960)
Contrary to the early 335 (and 345) equipped with a vibrato, the 355 did not exhibit a "Custom made" plaque, since it was fitted with such a device on quite a regular basis.

The 355 headstock featuring the split diamond inlay.

The control board of a 355 with Varitone.

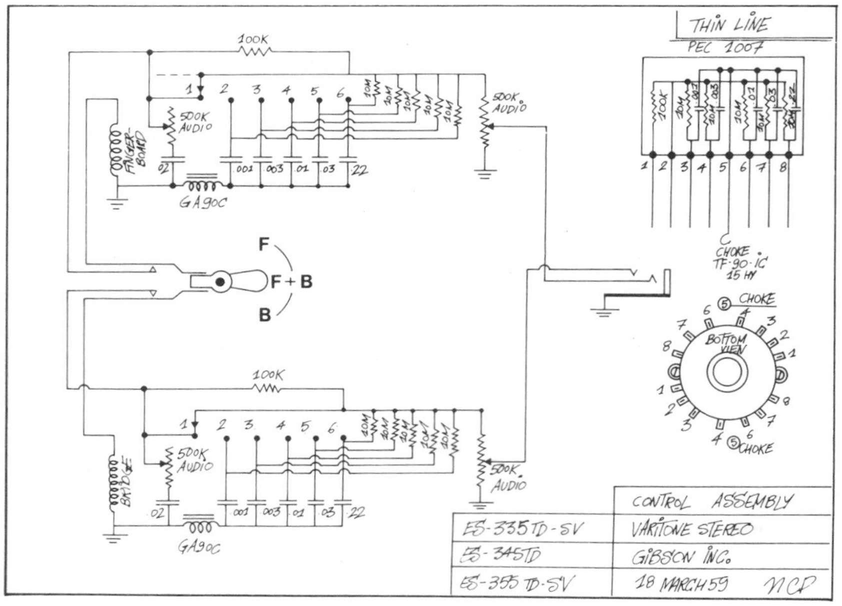


The Varitone circuitry perfected by Walt Fuller, as reprinted from the Gibson files.

The legendary BB King

1960 ES-355
equipped with the Gibson
"Sideways" Vibrola

A very unusual ES-355 with a flame maple top and a light Sunburst finish.

In May 1960, the Stereo model (ES-355 TD-SV) cost $ 600.00, while the Mono version was priced at $ 550.00.

# THE ES-345 TD

Another model appeared at the beginning of 1959 mounted in stereo with a Varitone, to fill the gap between the 335 and the 355 : it was the **ES-345 TD.** The letters "SV" were not retained, as theoretically no "mono" variant was available for this model. However a few 345's were offered around 1960 in "mono", mainly with a cherry finish according to the Gibson registers. The very first ES-345's were shipped in February 1959 (serial numbers A 29131 and on), and these examples were actually begun at the end of 1958 after the 355 had been launched.

Besides the Varitone, the 345 was characterized by its bound rosewood fingerboard with double parallelogram position markers (like an ES-175) starting at the 3rd fret. The headstock, on the other hand, resembled the 335's with the "crown" inlay while the metal parts were gold-plated like on an ES-355. Basically a 345 could be considered as a slightly fancier 335 equipped with the electrical hardware of a 355 (stereo model). However, the fingerboard of the 345 is somewhat narrower than the 335's with usually 41 mm at the nut and 51 mm at the 12th fret on the regular models of the late fifties.

Just like the 335 and the 355, the first 345's were equipped with a "long" scratch plate extending beyond the Tune-O-Matic bridge. The models which were factory equipped with a vibrato tailpiece had the same "Custom Made" plaque found on the 335 although a few guitars had pearl dots over the holes intended for the stop tailpiece. In 1959, the 345 was offered in "Sunburst" or "Natural", then starting in 1960, a "Cherry Red" finish was introduced and it soon replaced the "Natural" (or "Blonde") models whose last examples were actually shipped in 1960. This "Cherry Red" option was available on the 345 **after** the 355 but **before** the 335. A fourth choice was announced in the July-August 1960 issue of the "Gibson Gazette". It was "Argentine Grey" but very few models were actually made with this exceedingly rare finish, which was simply a black sunburst fading into pale yellow. Argentine Grey was offered on special order only and besides the 345, it was used on a few 335's and 355's as well as some Byrdlands. As regards the 345 no more than two or three dozens were finished this way between late 1959 (ES-345 TD with a number A 31848 noted in the Gibson books in December 1959) and 1961. As a matter of interest we have noticed on the few "Argentine Grey" models we came across that the rims were also finished with a sunburst and not plain as on a "regular" Sunburst 345.

In July 1960, the 345 was, therefore, available in four variants at the following prices :

| | |
|---|---|
| ES-345 TD (Sunburst) | : $ 365.00 |
| ES-345 TDC (Cherry) | : $ 380.00 |
| ES-345 TDN (Natural) | : $ 400.00 |
| ES-345 TDA (Argentine Grey) | : $ 400.00 |

Lastly, although it was never officially announced, it is known, a few 345's (and 335's) were finished around 1960 in a very unusual green-into-yellow Sunburst which was already in use on some Epiphone guitars (made by Gibson) at that time.

Very soon, however, the "Cherry" and "Sunburst" models were the only ones available, and they were produced in rather equal numbers. The 345 fitted in perfectly between the 335 and the 355 as it was manufactured in quantities smaller than the first one but greater than the second. Lastly the 345 followed the same evolution as the 335 concerning its body shape.

# THE EB-6 BASS

In 1960, Gibson proposed as a complement to the EB-2 in the semi-solid series a second bass model, this time with six strings, designated the **EB-6.** A 6-string bass is tuned one octave **below** a normal guitar and employs the same tuning (EADGBE). In the late fifties a trend for 6-string basses was beginning to develop among guitarists who also wanted to play bass, but differently from a regular bass player or with special effects. The EB-6 was widely inspired from the 4-string EB-2 with the same scale length (that is 30 1/2"), a 20 fret unbound

ES-345 TD (1961)
with a stop tailpiece and a "short" pick guard.

ES-345 TD (1960)
with a stop tailpiece and a " long " pick guard.

This 1959 ES-345 was factory equipped with a Bigsby vibrato tailpiece and consequently it sports a "Custom made"plaque.

fingerboard and a neck-to-body junction at the 18th fret. The combination bridge tailpiece was based on the same principle as the unit on the EB-2, with no adjustment string-by-string for intonation.

The EB-6 only had one special Humbucking bass pick-up similar in appearance to a normal guitar Humbucker. Like the EB-2, it had a volume and a tone control with a bass/baritone switch in order to broaden the tonal possibilities. The EB-6 resembled more a guitar than a bass, but it was possible to differentiate the EB-6 by its neck which was slightly longer. Otherwise the tuning machines and the overall appearance were similar to a one pick-up guitar.

The semi-solid EB-6 was only offered from 1960 up to about 1962, when the name was applied to a new "solid body" SG type model with **two** Humbucking pick-ups. The EB-6 was only available in "Sunburst" and in May 1960, it sold for $ 325.00 compared to $ 285 for an EB-2.

In 1960, the Gibson "semi-solid" line was composed of six models : 4 guitars — ES-335 TD, ES-345 TD, ES-355 TD, ES-355 TD-SV — and 2 basses — EB-2 and EB-6.

# THE ES-330 MODEL

Another model was, however, introduced as early as 1959 under the name **ES-330.** We have purposely ignored it so far, since despite its double cutaway shape, it was not a semi-solid guitar. Indeed the new ES-330 did not have a solid center block like the different models we have just examined.

The 330 was merely a "thin line" guitar similar in structure to an ES-225. Furthermore, its 22 fret neck was much more "sunk" into the body and joined at the 16th instead of at the 19th fret as on the 335, 345 and 355. This meant a receded positioning of the Tune-O-Matic bridge now at the same level as the middle of the "F" holes, while the large pick-guard extended only abreast with the back pick-up.

Nevertheless, taking its designation and its shape into account we have chosen to include the 330 in this chapter, although it was not actually a semi-solid guitar.

The body of the 330 was made entirely of maple, with a one piece mahogany neck and a bound rosewood fingerboard, fitted with pearl dot position markers. The Gibson logo was inlaid in pearl on the headstock, but the 330, however, did not have the crown design of the 335 or the 345. Lastly, it was equipped from the outset with a trapeze tailpiece and not a stop-tailpiece.

The combination of these few details gave the 330 a rather different aspect from the other semi-solid models, and at first glance, it is difficult to confuse it with a 335, although the 330 is often termed as the "poor man's dot neck guitar" !

From 1959, the 330 was offered either in a one or in a double pick-up version with a "Sunburst" or "Natural" finish. The pick-ups were single coil units with black plastic covers and surface mounting "ears". On the single pick-up model, designated ES-330 T or ES-330 TN according to the finish, the pick-up was located half-way between the bridge and the fingerboard like on the ES-225T.

In May 1960, the prices of these different models were as follows :

| | |
|---|---|
| ES-330 T | : $ 210.00 |
| ES-330 TN | : $ 225.00 |
| ES-330 TD | : $ 250.00 |
| ES-330 TDN | : $ 265.00 |

"Natural" was soon replaced by a "Cherry Red" finish starting in 1960, but both options were available during that year.

Later on, in the early 1960's, the single pick-up model was discontinued, and the last ES-330 T's and TC's were shipped in 1963. As for the double pick-up version, it was shown in the catalog until the 1970's.

Also around the end of 1962, the pearl dot inlays on the fingerboard were replaced by small rectangular blocks similar to the ones on the 335 of the same period, and the black plastic pick-up covers were changed for chrome covers.

The 330 was, numerically speaking, the biggest seller of the double cutaway series in the late fifties and early sixties even if it was not a real semi-solid guitar !

On the whole, the "semi-solid" series met a lively success throughout the 1960's and, its influence in the Gibson line did not show

ES 330 TD (1960)

ES 330 TDN (1960)
As typical of the early 330's, note pearl dot position markers and black plastic pick-up covers.
The Grover keys are not original.

A Blonde ES-330 T from 1959 with its single pick-up located half way between the fingerboard and the Tune-O-Matic bridge. Note neck-to-body junction at the 16th fret.

a decrease until the return of the Les Paul guitars in 1968.

The rounded double cutaway shape, characteristic of this series remains, aesthetically speaking, one of the most successful design of the Gibson line, and if one needs to be convinced of this fact, a simple count of all the different "adaptations" made by Gibson's competitors is all that is needed.

Furthermore, a host of Blues guitarists are associated with this type of guitar : BB King and his 355, nicknamed "Lucille", are just a perfect illustration like Elvin Bishop and his 345's.

As for Rock Chuck Berry has been using semi-solid guitars, no matter what the model, for most of his career. More recently, some very talented guitarists such as Larry Carlton, Lee Ritenour or John Scofield have shown their clear preference for this type of instrument whose versatility, allows them to tackle different styles of music particularly in a recording studio.

# TRANSITION

To many, the fifties are the Golden Era of the Electric guitar, especially for Gibson, because of the models which were introduced during this period. It is true that throughout this decade, the electric guitar saw a great number of innovations intimately linked to its soaring popularity and to the advent of new musical trends.

However it would be unwise in our opinion to "cherish" outrageously the 1950's productions, as several models — including the most sought after today — were moderately appreciated (to say the least !) at the time of their introduction. The original Les Paul series that was stopped by Gibson in early 1961 because of its waning popularity is a good example... since a 1960 Les Paul Standard is presently one of the most coveted electric guitar ! A somewhat subjective interpretation is always part of the story, but any survey aspiring to be as objective as possible cannot afford to rely upon the evaluation of today.

Nevertheless, it is quite true that the early sixties heralded a transition in the evolution of the company, and 1961, might be considered as a "turning point" in many respects, since at that time quite a few changes occured in the range itself as well as in the means of production. The first effects of a growing demand for electrics could already be felt, indeed, as early as 1958, but 1961 is somehow the year when changes actually started to materialize.

First, as regards the Gibson range, 1961 saw the introduction to the public of a new series of solid body guitars which, after carrying the Les Paul markings for nearly 3 years, became known as the "SG" series. The innovating design used for this new line was soon extended to other models such as four-string and six-string basses or double neck guitars which all received the typically sharp double cutaway shape.

During the sixties, the "SG" series and its derivatives were instrumental in having the solid body concept permanently accepted by a larger number of players.

The wild looking Firebirds and Thunderbirds introduced for the first time in 1963 opened up new vistas in guitar aesthetics and construction, with their full length laminated necks.

Starting in 1961, Gibson made available several "Artist" models carrying the names of performers who contributed to their design (... or simply endorsed them !). This new "galaxy of stars" soon included electric guitars named after Johnny Smith, Barney Kessel, Tal Farlow and Trini Lopez... as well as Richard Pick or the Everly Brothers on the acoustic side... It did show Gibson was really a professionnal guitar (intended for sale to "amateurs" however !). At the same time, electric acoustic models such a the Super 400-CES, L-5 CES, Byrdland, ES-350 T and ES-5 Switchmaster were revamped and as early as 1961 received a sharp Florentine cutaway in place of the original rounded Venetian Cutaway. Last but not least the sixties stood out as years of remarkable success for the all new semi-solid series introduced in 1958, but whose range was fully completed by 1960 only.

Besides these different changes in the Gibson electrics, 1961 was also the year when the production started to increase in quantities owing to an additional building erected on Parsons Street in 1960.

Thanks to the new-premises which nearly doubled the size of manufacturing facilities, the Gibson sales progressed at incredible rates during the sixties. This amazing growth is clearly reflected by the increase in sales which reached 650 % between 1949 and 1964 — with barely 250 % from 1949 to 1961 — while between 1964 and 1966 the turnover was simply doubled during what is currently termed at the first "guitar boom".

This unprecedented demand for guitars — both acoustic and electric — threw into confusion an industry which was not used to progress at such a pace. As Ted McCarty puts it with a smile ! "for us there was no ceiling !"

Finally, throughout the sixties, the image of the guitar markedly moved into the electric side to the detriment of the acoustic guitar whose audience, after the early sixties "folk boom" was somewhat restricted by rock'n roll or pop music... even Bob Dylan changed his horse to rock his poems in the course of the sixties ! then the seventies awarded an ever increasing supremacy to the electric guitar over its acoustic counterpart thanks to hard rock or more recently, to what some called "punk rock". New trends such as "fusion" music were also instrumental in assessing the importance of the electric instrument, while jazz, after a short eclipse, is now stronger than ever to make its voice heard with new talented and innovative players.

The second volume of Gibson Electrics will deal with the different stages of such a conquest between 1961 and 1981 and examine the different models which established the Gibson guitar on a pinacle.

# APPENDICES

*In order provide complementary information to the different chapters of this volume dealing with GIBSON ELECTRICS from their appearance up to 1961, we have gathered into three appendices some useful statistics and technical data.*

*It seemed to us that reference to these statistics would be more practical in the form of an easy to read chart or as regards identification numbers in a distinct paragraph.*

*The three appendices are the following :*

* *Appendix I presents the main specifications of the different electric models manufactured between 1936 and 1961, as well as the salient features in their evolution.*

* *Appendix II indicates, starting in 1948, the annual shipping totals of the most significant instruments of the period.*

* *Appendix III deals with the identification numbers – serial and factory numbers – used by Gibson from 1935 up to 1961 and analyses the major systems into operation during this period.*

# APPENDIX I
# SPECIFICATIONS OF THE GIBSON ELECTRICS
## introduced between 1936 and 1961

We have gathered in an easy-to-read chart the main specifications of the electric models examined throughout the different chapters of this book. However, for obvious reasons, we have only retained "stock" models with their original specifications, and all the "one of a kind" instruments were intentionally discarded. Any major evolution and/or salient features are shown in the column headed "Main Modifications".

Naturally, this chart could not contain "everything" regarding the detailed evolution of any Gibson guitar and it should be read in conjunction with the chapters concerning each model. Nevertheless it can provide a quick reference in order to check out a detail on a given instrument or compare, side by side, the specifications of different guitars.

On the other hand, it is necessary to keep in mind a few overall characteristics of the Gibson models over the years. Some of them, such as the different shades in the "Sunburst" finish are unfortunately difficult to explain and they require the experience of someone lucky enough to have seen a number of Gibson guitars, pass through his hands! Besides, photos showing Sunburst models are not always self explanatory since the conditions of the exposure can vary to a large extent and make a guitar look darker (or brighter) than it is actually.

To cut a long story short, the instruments of the thirties and forties usually have a "darker" sunburst finish than those of the fifties and more particularly of the late fifties, which had somewhat more red in their sunburst with clearer surroundings. Thus, the older Gibson electrics had a dark brown-into-yellow sunburst, which was then designated by the name of "cremona brown with a golden sunburst". Of course the nuance could vary to some extent with the wood used for the body, i.e. maple or spruce.

At this stage, it must be noted that the "economy" models only had a sunburst finish on top, whilst the back and sides were plain and dark (e.g. ES 125 or ES 225). The "intermediate" models, in turn, had a sunburst finish both on top and back with plain sides (e.g. ES 175 or ES 335). Last, but not least, the more expensive models offered a sunburst finish on the whole body, that is, top, back and sides, and even on the neck (e.g. SUPER 400 CES or ES 350).

In the late fifties the famed "Cherry Sunburst", i.e. "cherry red into yellow", was introduced on the legendary Les Paul Standard and then offered on other models such as the ES 125 TC. Meanwhile the regular standard finish was already clearer with a see-through "light brown-into-yellow" nuance. The old type sunburst finish was reintroduced much later, under the name "Tobacco Sunburst" in order to differentiate it from the regular finish.

As it can be see from the shipping totals (see Appendix II) guitars with a "Natural" or "Blonde" finish were actually manufactured in lesser quantities and they are, therefore, rarer than "Sunburst" models. "Natural" was even temporarily discontinued on several guitars, such as the ES 175 or the ES 335 on the threshold of the sixties.

These instruments were often made with flame or bird's eye maple and the "Natural" finish aptly revealed the quality of the wood.

Besides the finish "F" holes changed slightly over the years and they were definitely slenderer on the older models. As a matter of fact ever since 1936 they have not stopped getting bigger, owing to an increased mechanization. This is especially obvious on a model like the ES 175. By the way it must be stated that the old Les Paul's were manufactured with the use of carving machines and none of them were actually hand-made ! A change in the contour body was later brought about by a simple change of machinery.

Before the Second World War the necks often presented a markedly triangular section which, however, turned quickly to a rounder profile. A 1941 ES 300, for instance, may have a perfectly round and "clubby" neck. It did remain so until 1960 when the necks started to become flatter and also wider in a lot of cases (e.g. ES 335 or ES 350 T). It is not until 1963 that the bottom of the neck started to get somewhat thicker around the heel. Up to 1961, most of the necks were made from one piece of Honduras mahogany on the "regular" and even on a few top models such as the Les Paul Custom or the ES 355. The more luxurious instruments had a laminated (2 piece) curly maple neck with a dark wood seam in the middle.

Gibson used a rather thin fretwire on all of its models until 1959, then wider frets -often nicknamed jumbo frets-were introduced and soon adopted on several guitars with the exception of models such as the Les Paul custom. Consequently, a 1954 Les Paul model with wide frets could only be a refretted instrument.

For the period we are interested in, metal parts were either "gold plated" (... not very lasting by all standards !) on the more expensive models, or "nickel plated". Chrome plated metal parts — look for a "blue" reflection instead of a "yellow" one as on nickel plating — were not introduced until the mid. sixties.

From a purely aesthetic viewpoint, different knobs were used by Gibson between 1936 and 1961. Of course this detail can easily be counterfeited — especially with Japanese parts or even Gibson's own reissues — however, the illustration included in this appendix, shows the types of knobs used from 1940 up to 1960. Unfortunately we could not find, at the time this photo was taken, a sample of the old Charlie Christian knob which looked like a round chocolate toffee with an arrow pointer !

As a matter of fact, a number of subtleties allow the genuineness of an instrument to be ascertained, or cross checked to see whether it is actually what it is claimed to be. All these details call, once more, for a basic knowledge of the Gibson guitar and for... experience ! In any case, they are not of an essential historic interest, except for a hard-core "GIBSON-ITE" or a collector.

Lastly, as regards pick-ups, we have not mentioned their specifications in the chart since the question was covered in details throughout the chapters. The chart including the specifications of the Gibson electrics introduced between 1936 and 1961 is divided in three parts according to the type of the instruments : acoustic, solid-body and semi-solid. Each model is introduced in chronological order.

We have gathered in this photograph the different knobs featured on the Gibson models between 1940 and 1960 with, from left to right, the type used :
— in the early forties
— after the War until about 1949
— from 1949 up to early 1953 (with numbers from 0 to 10 for the first time, these knobs are often nicknamed "hatknobs" or "barrel knobs"
— from 1953 up to mid-1955 (slightly lower than the previous type, they are sometimes called "speed" knobs)
— from 1955 up to mid-1960 (sometimes known as "bonnet" knobs)
— starting in 1960 (with a metal cap indicating "tone" or "volume").
The numbered knobs were available in gold and black tinted plastic depending upon the model they were intended for while on the EB-1 they were brown.

## ELECTRIC ACOUSTIC GUITARS

| MODEL | Type | Intro-duced in | No. of pick ups | Type of pick ups | Dimensions w × l × d (in inches) | Cutaway | Scale length (in inches) | No. of frets | Ne E jur ( |
|---|---|---|---|---|---|---|---|---|---|
| **ES 150 (Electric Spanish)** | Acoustic | 1936 | 1 | Single coil (Bar p.u.) | 16 1/4 × 20 1/4 × 3 3/8 | No | 24 3/4 | 19 | |
| **ES 100** | Acoustic | 1938 | 1 | Single coil (Bar p.u.) | 14 3/4 × 19 1/4 × 3 3/8 | No | 24 3/4 | 19 | |
| **ES 250** | Acoustic | 1940 | 1 | Single coil (Bar p.u.) | 17 × 21 × 3 3/8 | No | 25 1/2 | 19 | |
| **ES 300** | Acoustic | 1940 | 1 | Single coil | 17 × 21 × 3 3/8 | No | 25 1/2 | 20 | |
| **ES 125** | Acoustic | 1941 | 1 | Single coil | 14 3/4 × 19 1/4 × 3 3/8 | No | 24 3/4 | 19 | |
| **ES 350** | Acoustic | 1947 | 1 | Single coil | 17 × 21 × 3 3/8 | Yes Venetian | 25 1/2 | 20 | |
| **L 7 E ED** | Acoustic | 1948 | 1 or 2 | Single coil | 17 × 21 × 3 3/8 | No | 25 1/2 | 20 | |
| **L 7 PE PED** | Acoustic | 1948 | 1 or 2 | Single coil | 17 × 21 × 3 3/8 | Yes Venetian | 25 1/2 | 20 | |
| **ES 175** | Acoustic | 1949 | 1 | Single coil | 16 1/4 × 20 1/4 × 3 3/8 | Yes Florentine | 24 3/4 | 19 | |
| **ES 5** | Acoustic | 1949 | 3 | Single coil | 17 × 21 × 3 3/8 | Yes Venitian | 25 1/2 | 19 | |
| **ES 140 three quarter size model** | Acoustic | 1950 | 1 | Single coil | 12 3/4 × 17 1/4 × 3 3/8 | Yes Florentine | 22 3/4 | 19 | |
| **CF-100 E** | Flat top acoustic | 1951 | 1 | Single coil | 14 1/4 × 19 × 4 3/8 | Yes Florentine | 24 3/4 | 19 | |
| **L 5 CES** | Acoustic | 1951 | 2 | Single coil | 17 × 21 × 3 3/8 | Yes Venitian | 25 1/2 | 20 | |
| **SUPER 400 CES** | Acoustic | 1951 | 2 | Single coil | 18 × 21 3/4 × 3 3/8 | Yes Venitian | 25 1/2 | 20 | |
| **ES 295** | Acoustic | 1952 | 2 | Single coil | 16 1/4 × 20 1/4 × 3 3/8 | Yes Florentine | 24 3/4 | 19 | |
| **ES 175 D** | Acoustic | 1953 | 2 | Single coil | 16 1/4 × 20 1/4 × 3 3/8 | Yes Florentine | 24 3/4 | 19 | |

| board e of | Neck made of | Body made of | Standard finish | MAIN MODIFICATIONS (up to 1961) | Eventually discontinued in |
|---|---|---|---|---|---|
| wood | One piece mahogany | Spruce top with maple back and sides | Golden Sunburst on top only | Bar pick up withdrawn in 1940 and replaced by new single coil unit near the bridge from 1940 up to 1942. Enlarged body (17" × 21") with laminated maple top starting in 1945. Pick up at the end of the fingerboard. 20 frets instead of 19. | 1955 |
| wood | One piece mahogany | Spruce top with maple back and sides | Golden Sunburst on top only | Bar pick up withdrawn in 1940 and replaced by new single coil unit near the bridge in 1940 and 1941. | 1941 |
| wood | Laminated maple | Spruce top with maple back and sides | Sunburst | | 1940 |
| wood | Laminated maple | Spruce top with maple back and sides | Natural | Large diagonal pick up withdrawn in early 1941 and replaced by smaller diagonal unit located near the bridge in 1941 and 1942. Available in Sunburst starting in 1941. Laminated maple top with pick up at the end of the fingerboard after the war. Fitted with 2 pick ups and 3 controls starting in 1948. | 1952 ① |
| wood | One piece mahogany | Spruce top with maple back and sides | Golden Sunburst on top only | Enlarged body (16 1/4" × 20 1/4") with laminated maple top and mahogany back and sides after the war. Pick up at the end of the fingerboard. Trapezoidal position markers up to 1950, then dot inlay. Maple back. 20 fret fingerboard starting in 1955. | 1969 |
| wood | Laminated maple | Laminated maple, top, back and sides | Sunburst or Natural (ES 350 N) | Fitted with 2 pick ups and 3 controls starting in 1948. Equipped with independant volume and tone controls for each pick up around 1952. | 1956 |
| wood | Laminated maple | Spruce top with maple back and sides | Sunburst | Natural finish available as from 1950. | 1952 |
| wood | Laminated maple | Spruce top with maple back and sides | Sunburst | Name changed to L7 CE and L7 CED in 1949. Natural finish available as from 1950. | 1954 ② |
| wood | One piece mahogany | Laminated maple top, back and sides | Sunburst or Natural (ES 175 N) | 20 fret fingerboard starting in 1955. Humbucking pick up replaced single coil unit in 1957. Fitted with a fancier tail piece around 1958. | 1972 |
| wood | Laminated maple | Laminated maple top, back and sides | Sunburst or Natural (ES 5 N) | See ES 5 Switchmaster. | 1955 |
| wood | One piece mahogany | Laminated maple, top, back and sides | Sunburst | Natural finish available only in 1956. Replaced by "thin line" version introduced in 1956. | 1957 |
| wood | One piece mahogany | Laminated spruce top mahogany back and sides | Golden Sunburst on top only | 20 fret fingerboard starting in 1955. | 1959 |
| ony | Laminated maple | Spruce top with solid maple back and sides | Sunburst or Natural (L 5 CESN) | Fitted with Humbucking pick ups around late 1957. Sharp florentine cutaway starting at the end of 1960. | Current model |
| ony | Laminated maple | Spruce top with solid maple back and sides | Sunburst or Natural (S 400 CESN) | Fitted with Humbucking pick ups around late 1957. Sharp florentine cutaway starting at the end of 1960. | Current model |
| wood | One piece mahogany | Laminated maple back and sides | All Gold finish | 20 fret fingerboard starting in 1955. | 1958 |
| wood | One piece mahogany | Laminated maple back and sides | Sunburst or Natural (ES 175 DN) | 20 fret fingerboard starting in 1955. Fitted with Humbucking pick ups in 1957. Equipped with fancier tail piece around 1958. | Current model |

## ELECTRIC ACOUSTIC GUITARS

| MODEL | Type | Intro-duced in | No. of pick ups | Type of pick ups | Dimensions w × l × d (in inches) | Cutaway | Scale length (in inches) | No. of frets | Nc I ju ( |
|---|---|---|---|---|---|---|---|---|---|
| **J-160 E** | Flat top acoustic | 1954 | 1 | Single coil | 16 1/4 × 20 1/4 × 4 7/8 | No | 24 3/4 | 19 | |
| **ES 135** | Acoustic | 1954 | 1 | Single coil | 16 1/4 × 20 1/4 × 3 3/8 | No | 24 3/4 | 19 | |
| **ES 5 Switchmaster** | Acoustic | 1955 | 3 | Single coil | 17 × 21 × 3 3/8 | Yes Venitian | 25 1/2 | 20 | |
| **ES 225 T** | Thin line acoustic | 1955 | 1 | Single coil | 16 1/4 × 20 1/4 × 1 3/4 | Yes Florentine | 24 3/4 | 20 | |
| **BYRDLAND** | Thin line acoustic | 1955 | 2 | Single coil (Alnico) | 17 × 21 × 2 1/4 | Yes Venitian | 23 1/2 | 22 | |
| **ES 350 T** | Thin line acoustic | 1955 | 2 | Single coil | 17 × 21 × 2 1/4 | Yes Venitian | 23 1/2 | 22 | |
| **ES 225 TD** | Thin line acoutic | 1956 | 2 | Single coil | 16 1/4 × 20 1/4 × 1 3/4 | Yes Florentine | 24 3/4 | 20 | |
| **ES 140 T three quarter size model** | Thin line acoustic | 1956 | 1 | Single coil | 12 3/4 × 17 1/4 × 1 3/4 | Yes Florentine | 22 3/4 | 19 | |
| **ES 125 T** | Thin line acoustic | 1956 | 1 | Single coil | 16 1/4 × 20 1/4 × 1 3/4 | No | 24 3/4 | 20 | |
| **ES 125 TD** | Thin line acoustic | 1957 | 2 | Single coil | 16 1/4 × 20 1/4 × 1 3/4 | No | 24 3/4 | 20 | |
| **ES 125 T three quarter size model** | Thin line acoustic | 1957 | 1 | Single coil | 12 3/4 × 17 1/4 × 1 3/4 | No | 22 3/4 | 19 | |
| **DOUBLE 12** | Acoustic (without sound hole) | 1958 | 2 + 2 | Humbucking | 17 1/4 × 20 × 1 7/8 | Yes double florentine | 24 3/4 (each neck) | 20 | |
| **DOUBLE MANDOLIN** | Acoustic (without sound hole) | 1958 | 1 + 2 | Humbucking | 17 1/4 × 20 × 1 7/8 | Yes double florentine | 13 7/8 (mandolin) 24 3/4 (guitar) | 24 20 | ( ( |
| **ES 330 T** | Thin line acoustic | 1959 | 1 | Single coil | 16 × 19 × 1 3/4 | Yes double rounded | 24 3/4 | 22 | |
| **ES 330 TD** | Thin line acoustic | 1959 | 2 | Single coil | 16 × 19 × 1 3/4 | Yes double rounded | 24 3/4 | 22 | |
| **ES 125 TC** | Thin line acoustic | 1960 | 1 | Single coil | 16 1/4 × 20 1/4 × 1 3/4 | Yes Florentine | 24 3/4 | 20 | |
| **ES 125 TCD** | Thin line acoustic | 1960 | 2 | Single coil | 16 1/4 × 20 1/4 × 1 3/4 | Yes Florentine | 24 3/4 | 20 | |
| **C-1 E** | Flat top acoustic | 1960 | 1 | Ceramic | 14 1/4 × 19 × 4 1/2 | No | 25 1/2 | 19 | |

| er board ade of | Neck made of | Body made of | Standard finish | MAIN MODIFICATIONS (up to 1961) | Eventually discontinued in |
|---|---|---|---|---|---|
| ewood | One piece mahogany | spruce top mahogany back and sides | Golden Sunburst on top only | 20 fret fingerboard starting in 1955. New style pick guard fitted around 1958. | 1977 |
| ewood | One piece mahogany | maple top and back, mahogany sides | Golden Sunburst on top only | 20 fret fingerboard starting in 1955. | 1958 |
| ewood | Laminated maple | maple top, back and sides | Sunburst or Natural | Fancier tailpiece fitted in 1956. Humbucking pick ups in late 1957. Sharp cutaway by the end of 1960. | 1961 |
| ewood | One piece mahogany | maple top back and sides | Golden Sunburst on top only | Natural finish available starting in 1956 only. | 1959 |
| bony | Laminated maple | Spruce top with solid maple back and sides | Sunburst or Natural (N) | Humbucking pick ups fitted around late 1957 with new black pick guard. Sharp florentine cutaway by the end of 1960. | Current model |
| ewood | Laminated maple | maple top back and sides | Sunburst or Natural | Humbucking pick ups fitted around late 1957. Sharp florentine cutaway by the end of 1960. | 1963 ③ |
| sewood | One piece mahogany | maple top, back and sides | Sunburst or Natural | | 1959 |
| sewood | One piece mahogany | maple top back and sides | Sunburst or Natural | Natural finish not available after 1958. | 1970 |
| sewood | One piece mahogany | maple top and back, mahogany sides | Sunburst | A few models made with four controls and a toggle switch for one pick up. | 1969 |
| sewood | One piece mahogany | maple top and back, mahogany sides | Sunburst | | 1963 |
| sewood | One piece mahogany | maple top and back, mahogany sides | Sunburst | | 1968 |
| sewood | One piece mahogany | Spruce top, maple back and sides | Sunburst or solid white or solid black | | 1967 ④ |
| sewood | One piece mahogany | Spruce top maple back and sides | Sunburst or solid white or solid black | | 1967 ⑤ |
| sewood | One piece mahogany | maple top, back and sides | Sunburst or Natural | Cherry red finish available starting in 1960. Natural finish not available after 1960. | 1963 |
| sewood | One piece mahogany | maple top, back and sides | Sunburst or Natural | Cherry red finish available starting in 1960. Natural finish not available after 1960. | 1972 |
| sewood | One piece mahogany | maple top, back and sides | Cherry Sunburst | | 1970 |
| sewood | One piece mahogany | maple top, back and sides | Cherry Sunburst | Name changed to ES 125 TDC in 1961. | 1970 |
| sewood | One piece mahogany | Spruce top mahogany back and sides | Natural spruce top and mahogany back and sides | | 1968 |

## SOLID BODY GUITARS AND BASSES

| MODEL | Type | Intro-duced in | No. of pick ups | Type of pick ups | Dimensions w × l × d (in inches) | Cutaway | Scale length (in inches) | No. of frets | Nec B jun (f |
|---|---|---|---|---|---|---|---|---|---|
| **LES PAUL model (Standard)** | Solid body | 1952 | 2 | Single coil | 12 3/4 × 17 1/4 × 1 3/4 | Yes | 24 3/4 | 22 | 1 |
| **ELECTRIC BASS EB-1** | Solid body bass | 1953 | 1 | Single coil | 11 1/2 × 19 × 2 | — | 30 1/2 | 20 | 1 |
| **LES PAUL Custom** | Solid body | 1954 | 2 | Single coil | 12 3/4 × 17 1/4 × 1 3/4 | Yes | 24 3/4 | 22 | 1 |
| **LES PAUL Junior** | Solid body | 1954 | 1 | Single coil | 12 3/4 × 17 1/4 × 1 3/4 | Yes | 24 3/4 | 22 | 1 |
| **LES PAUL TV** | Solid body | 1954 | 1 | Single coil | 12 3/4 × 17 1/4 × 1 3/4 | Yes | 24 3/4 | 22 | 1 |
| **LES PAUL Special** | Solid body | 1955 | 2 | Single coil | 12 3/4 × 17 1/4 × 1 3/4 | Yes | 24 3/4 | 22 | 1 |
| **LES PAUL Junior "3/4" Three quarter size model** | Solid body | 1956 | 1 | Single coil | 12 3/4 × 17 1/4 × 1 3/4 | Yes | 22 3/4 | 19 | 1 |
| **FLYING V** | Solid body | 1958 | 2 | Humbucking | 4 1/2 × 19 1/2 × 1 1/2<br>16 3/4 | — | 24 3/4 | 22 | 2 |
| **EXPLORER** | Solid body | 1958 | 2 | Humbucking | 16 1/4 × 22 × 1 1/2 | Yes | 24 3/4 | 22 | 1 |
| **LES PAUL Special "3/4" Three quarter size model** | Solid body | 1959 | 2 | Single coil | 12 3/4 × 17 1/4 × 1 3/4 | Yes double cutaway | 22 3/4 | 19 | 1 |
| **EB-O** | Solid body bass | 1959 | 1 | Humbucking | 13 × 16 1/2 × 1 3/4 | Yes double cutaway | 30 1/2 | 20 | be 1 |
| **MELODY MAKER (MM)** | Solid body | 1959 | 1 | Single coil | 12 3/4 × 17 1/4 × 1 3/8 | Yes | 24 3/4 | 22 | 1 |
| **MELODY MAKER "3/4" Three quarter size model** | Solid body | 1959 | 1 | Single coil | 12 3/4 × 17 1/4 × 1 3/8 | Yes | 22 3/4 | 19 | 1 |
| **SG TV** | Solid body | 1960 | 1 | Single coil | 12 3/4 × 17 1/4 × 1 3/4 | Yes double cutaway | 24 3/4 | 22 | 2 |
| **SG SPECIAL (SG-R SG-C)** | Solid body | 1960 | 2 | Single coil | 12 3/4 × 17 1/4 × 1 3/4 | Yes double cutaway | 24 3/4 | 22 | 2 |
| **SG Special "3/4" Three quarter size model** | Solid body | 1960 | 2 | Single coil | 12 3/4 × 17 1/4 × 1 3/4 | Yes double cutaway | 22 3/4 | 19 | 1 |
| **MELODY MAKER-D (MM-D)** | Solid body | 1960 | 2 | Single coil | 12 3/4 × 17 1/4 × 1 3/8 | Yes | 24 3/4 | 22 | 1 |

| er board ade of | Neck made of | Body made of | Standard finish | MAIN MODIFICATIONS (up to 1961) | Eventually discontinued in |
|---|---|---|---|---|---|
| sewood | One piece mahogany | Mahogany body with solid carved maple top | Gold top with mahogany back and sides | Les Paul trapeze bridge-tailpiece replaced by a "stud" tail piece in late 1953. Tune-O-Matic bridge in late 1955. Humbucking pick ups starting in 1957. New Cherry Sunburst finish during 1958 | 1963 ⑥ |
| sewood | One piece mahogany | Mahogany | Natural finish | | 1958 ⑦ |
| bony | One piece mahogany | Mahogany | Black finish | Fitted with 3 Humbucking pick ups in late 1957. Fitted with the new "SG style" sharp double cutaway body in 1961. | 1963 ⑧ |
| sewood | One piece mahogany | Mahogany | Golden Sunburst on top only with mahogany back and sides | New double cutaway shape with Cherry red finish introduced in 1958. Fitted with the new "SG style" sharp double cutaway body in 1961. | 1963 ⑨ |
| sewood | One piece mahogany | Mahogany | Limed mahogany | New double cutaway shape (similar to Les Paul Junior) introduced in 1958. Name changed to SG "TV" by the end of 1959. | 1960 |
| sewood | One piece mahogany | Mahogany | Limed mahogany | New double cutaway shape by the end of 1958 Name changed to SG-R and SG-C Special by the end of 1959. | 1960 ⑩ |
| sewood | One piece mahogany | Mahogany | Golden Sunburst on top only with mahogany back and sides | New double cutaway shape with Cherry red finish introduced in 1958. | 1961 |
| sewood | One piece Korina | Korina (2 pieces) | Natural | | 1959 ⑪ |
| sewood | One piece Korina | Korina | Natural | Early models with a "V" shaped headstock soon replaced by scimitar peg head. | 1959 ⑫ |
| sewood | One piece mahogany | Mahogany | Cherry red | Name changed to "SG special 3/4" by the end of 1959. | 1960 |
| sewood | One piece mahogany | Mahogany | Cherry red | Fitted with the new "SG style" sharp double cutaway body in 1961. | 1974 |
| sewood | One piece mahogany | Mahogany | Golden Sunburst on top only with mahogany back and sides | New symetrical double cutaway shape — based upon the original design — introduced in 1961 (not SG style). | 1970 |
| sewood | One piece mahogany | Mahogany | Golden Sunburst on top only with mahogany back and sides | New symetrical double cutaway shape — based upon the original design — introduced in 1961 (not SG style). | 1970 |
| sewood | One piece mahogany | Mahogany | Limed mahogany | Fitted with the new "SG style" sharp double cutaway body in 1961. | 1968 |
| sewood | One piece mahogany | Mahogany | Cherry red or Limed mahogany (cream finish) | Fitted with the new "SG style" sharp double cutaway body in 1961. | 1976 |
| sewood | One piece mahogany | Mahogany | Cherry red | | 1961 |
| sewood | One piece mahogany | Mahogany | Golden Sunburst on top only with mahogany back and sides | New symetrical double cutaway shape — based upon the original design — introduced in 1961 (not SG style). | 1970 ⑬ |

## SEMI SOLID GUITARS AND BASSES

| MODEL | Type | Intro-duced in | No. of pick ups | Type of pick ups | Dimensions w × l × d (in inches) | Cutaway | Scale length (in inches) | No. of frets | Nc I ju ( |
|---|---|---|---|---|---|---|---|---|---|
| **ES 335 T** | Semi solid | 1958 | 2 | Humbucking | 16 × 19 × 1 3/4 | Yes double rounded | 24 3/4 | 22 | 1 |
| **EB 2** | Semi solid bass | 1958 | 1 | Humbucking | 16 × 19 × 1 3/4 | Yes double rounded | 30 1/2 | 20 | 1 |
| **ES 355 T (MONO)** | Semi solid | 1958 | 2 | Humbucking | 16 × 19 × 1 3/4 | Yes double rounded | 24 3/4 | 22 | 1 |
| **ES 355 T (STEREO)** | Semi solid | 1959 | 2 | Humbucking | 16 × 19 × 1 3/4 | Yes double rounded | 24 3/4 | 22 | 1 |
| **ES 345 T** | Semi solid | 1959 | 2 | Humbucking | 16 × 19 × 1 3/4 | Yes double rounded | 24 3/4 | 22 | 1 |
| **EB 6** | Semi solid bass | 1960 | 1 | Humbucking | 16 × 19 × 1 3/4 | Yes double rounded | 30 1/2 | 20 | 1 |

## NOTES ON THE CHARTS

(1) — A few left-over ES 300's were shipped from the factory in early 1953.

(2) — According to the company's ledgers, no L 7 CE's were actually shipped in 1953.

(3) — In 1977 Gibson introduced a reissue of the venetian cutaway ES 350 T with two humbucking pick-ups. However this new edition was offered with a 25 1/2" scale length instead of 23 1/2".

(4) (5) — According to the company's ledgers the last double-neck models were shipped in 1967. However, they remained in the Gibson price lists until 1970, hence it is quite possible that some of them were actually made during this period on a custom order basis.
In 1975 a limited edition of the EDS 1275 (double twelve) was offered by Gibson. Then starting in 1978 it was again offered as a regular item.

(6) — Starting in 1961 the Les Paul markings were applied to a new model with a sharp double cutaway and a thinner body. Then, by the end of 1963 the Les Paul markings were withdrawn and the new guitar took the "SG" designation (SG : solid guitar). Thus, the Les Paul Standard became the "SG Standard".
In 1968, the original Les Paul series with a single cutaway body was reintroduced by Gibson owing to the popularity of the older models on the second hand market.

(7) — A reissue of the EB 1 was offered by Gibson as a limited edition in 1970 and 1971, albeit with slightly altered specifications and a chrome pick-up cover.

(8) — See 6.
The very last original Les Paul Custom's with an all mahogany body and a single cutaway were shipped in early 1961.
The new double cutaway Les Paul Custom introduced in 1961 was renamed "SG Custom" by the end of 1963.
In 1968 the single cutaway model was reintroduced albeit with a maple carved top and two humbuckers instead of three.

(9) — See 6.
The new double cutaway Les Paul Junior introduced in 1961 was renamed "SG junior" by the end of 1963.
The "Les Paul junior" has never been reintroduced by Gibson.

| er board ade of | Neck made of | Body made of | Standard finish | MAIN MODIFICATIONS (up to 1961) | Eventually discontinued in |
|---|---|---|---|---|---|
| ewood | One piece mahogany | Laminated maple top back and sides with maple central block | Sunburst or Natural (ES 335 TN) | Name changed to ES 335 TD around 1960. Cherry finish available in 1960 and Natural finish discontinued after 1960. Smaller pick guard fitted by the end of 1960. | Current model |
| ewood | One piece mahogany | Laminated maple top back and sides with maple central block | Sunburst or Natural (EB-2 N) | Fitted with barytone switch starting in 1959. Natural finish not available after 1960. | 1970 (14) |
| bony | One piece mahogany | Laminated maple top back and sides with maple central block | Cherry red | Name changed to ES 355 TD around 1960. Starting in 1960 the Bigsby vibrato tailpiece was replaced by the new Gibson Sideways Vibrola. However Bigsby tailpiece remained available as an optional equipment. Smaller pick guard fitted by the end of 1960. | 1970 |
| bony | One piece mahogany | Laminated maple top back and sides with maple central block | Cherry red | Name changed to ES 355 TD-SV around 1960. Starting in 1960 the Bigsby vibrato tailpiece was replaced by the new Gibson Sideways Vibrola. However Bigsby tailpiece remained available as an optional equipment. Smaller pick guard fitted by the end of 1960. | Current model |
| sewood | One piece mahogany | Laminated maple top back and sides with maple central block | Sunburst or Natural (ES-345 TN) | Name changed to ES 345 TD around 1960. Cherry finish available in 1960 and Natural finish discontinued after 1960. Smaller pick guard fitted by the end of 1960. | Current model |
| sewood | One piece mahogany | Laminated maple top back and sides with maple central block | Sunburst | In 1962 the semi-solid EB-6 was replaced by a solid body 6 string bass with a "SG style" body and two Humbucking pick ups. | 1962 |

(10) — In 1974, a reissue of the original single cutaway Les Paul Special was offered by Gibson as a limited edition with a dark sunburst finish instead of the original limed mahogany finish.
In 1977, the model was reintroduced as a regular item under the designation "Les Paul 55" with a tune-O-Matic bridge. The same year, Gibson made available a reissue of the 1959/1960 double cutaway Special also with a Tune-O-Matic bridge.

(11) — A few original Flying V's with a Korina body were actually shipped in 1962 and 1963.
The model was subsequently reintroduced as a limited edition in 1966/1967, 1970/1971, 1975 and thereafter. However all these reissues can be easily distinguished from the original model thanks to their mahogany body and a number of modifications.

(12) — A few original Explorer's with a Korina body were also shipped in 1962 and 1963, albeit in a larger quantity than Flying V's although the accurate figures are not available.
Starting in 1976 an Explorer reissue was offered by Gibson with a mahogany body.

(13) — In 1977 a reissue of the 1961/1963 double cutaway Melody Maker was introduced by Gibson with a Tune-O-Matic bridge.

(14) — No EB 2's were manufactured in 1962 and 1963, however the model was reintroduced by Gibson as a regular item in 1963. It was definitely discontinued in 1970. A two pick-up version was offered starting in 1966 under the designation EB 2 D.

# APPENDIX II
# PRODUCTION SHIPPING TOTALS

Thanks to the Gibson factory (and more especially to Ken Killman) we were able to obtain the production shipping totals for most of the electric guitars featured in this book. Thus the figures we are providing are to be considered as **the official Gibson figures** since they were extracted from the plant's own records. They clearly show the exact quantities dispatched each year, model by model, from 1948 up to 1961.

Such shipping totals allow for a better assessment of the rarity of certain models, and firmly establish the availability of an instrument at a given date. However one must bear in mind that a guitar shipped (for instance) in 1957 may well have been started as early as 1956 or even carry a 1956 serial number. The lapse of time required for the making of an instrument, as well as for quality controls or a temporary stocking results in a gap between the moment the manufacturing process starts and the date the instrument is actually shipped to a Gibson agent.

Likewise some models were shipped from the factory after the decision to stop them was taken, simply because they were under process or already held in stock. As an example a few ES 350's were shipped in 1956, although the new "thin line" ES 350 T — which was to replace the ES 350 in the Gibson range — had been introduced as early as 1955.

Of course, the absence of any figure in a column for a particular model means that no instrument of that type was shipped during the year in question. This doesn't imply that a prototype had not been already completed for experimental purposes, since we understand these totals only deal with guitars meant for the buying public.

Most of these figures have never been published before and we are satisfied they are of great interest to Gibson enthusiasts as several guitars are casually termed "rare" without proper evidence.

In order to make an easier reading of these statistics, we have divided the totals in 3 categories, namely "electric-acoustic", "solid body" and "thin-line" (combined with semi solid guitars).

# SHIPPING TOTALS

## ELECTRIC ACOUSTIC GUITARS (with full depth body)

| | 1948 | 1949 | 1950 | 1951 | 1952 | 1953 | 1954 | 1955 | 1956 | 1957 | 1958 | 1959 | 1960 | 1961 |
|---|---|---|---|---|---|---|---|---|---|---|---|---|---|---|
| **ES 300** | 190 | 76 | 116 | 114 | 79 | 4 | — | — | — | — | — | — | — | — |
| **ES 300 N** | 83 | 48 | 41 | 47 | 27 | — | — | — | — | — | — | — | — | — |
| **ES 350** | 87 | 76 | 54 | 70 | 122 | 87 | 58 | 44 | 45 | — | — | — | — | — |
| **ES 350 N** | 55 | 89 | 46 | 57 | 67 | 50 | 31 | 14 | 4 | — | — | — | — | — |
| **ES 5** | — | 66 | 111 | 88 | 126 | 72 | 65 | 45 | 4 | — | — | — | — | — |
| **ES 5 N** | — | 22 | 52 | 77 | 93 | 53 | 23 | 11 | — | — | — | — | — | — |
| **ES 5 SW** | — | — | — | — | — | — | — | 7 | 59 | 56 | 55 | 70 | 46 | 41 |
| **ES 5 N SW** | — | — | — | — | — | — | — | — | 39 | 30 | 34 | 33 | 20 | 11 |
| **ES 175** | — | 129 | 503 | 559 | 818 | 829 | 599 | 485 | 560 | 353 | 211 | 301 | 226 | 160 |
| **ES 175 N** | — | 13 | 30 | 105 | 192 | 181 | 141 | 115 | 146 | 92 | 66 | — | 5 | — |
| **ES 175 D** | — | — | — | — | — | 182 | 275 | 308 | 320 | 271 | 285 | 324 | 345 | 406 |
| **ES 175 DN** | — | — | — | — | — | 86 | 129 | 143 | 247 | 175 | 114 | 129 | 111 | 81 |
| **Super 400 CES** | — | — | — | 2 | 7 | 16 | 17 | 5 | 20 | 24 | 15 | 22 | 24 | 30 |
| **Super 400 CES N** | — | — | — | — | 11 | 11 | 6 | 16 | 19 | 15 | 15 | 8 | 7 | 15 |
| **L 5 CES** | — | — | — | 31 | 29 | 25 | 30 | 19 | 23 | 22 | 21 | 26 | 45 | 22 |
| **L 5 CES N** | — | — | — | 8 | 17 | 18 | 20 | 31 | 32 | 15 | 27 | 12 | 17 | 13 |
| **ES 295** | — | — | — | — | 297 | 637 | 357 | 166 | 193 | 71 | 49 | — | — | — |
| **CF 100 E** | — | — | — | 241 | 250 | 164 | 111 | 103 | 132 | 117 | 84 | 55 | — | — |
| **J 160 E** | — | — | — | — | — | — | 456 | 487 | 377 | 286 | 187 | 179 | 144 | 141 |
| **ES 140** | — | — | 393 | 307 | 264 | 409 | 367 | 244 | 354 | 17 | — | — | — | — |
| **ES 140 N** | — | — | — | — | — | — | — | — | 30 | — | — | — | — | — |
| **C 1 E** | — | — | — | — | — | — | — | — | — | — | — | — | 42 | 135 |

# SHIPPING TOTALS

## SOLID-BODY ELECTRIC GUITARS AND BASSES

| | 1950 | 1951 | 1952 | 1953 | 1954 | 1955 | 1956 | 1957 | 1958 | 1959 | 1960 | 1961 |
|---|---|---|---|---|---|---|---|---|---|---|---|---|
| **Les Paul Model and Standard** | — | — | 1.716 | 2.245 | 1.504 | 862 | 920 | 598 | 434 | 643 | 635 | 1.662* |
| **Les Paul Custom** | — | — | — | — | 94 | 355 | 489 | 283 | 256 | 246 | 189 | 513* |
| **Les Paul Junior** | — | — | — | — | 823 | 2.839 | 3.129 | 2.959 | 2.408 | 4.364 | 2.513 | 2.151* |
| **Les Paul TV (SG)** | — | — | — | — | 5 | 230 | 511 | 552 | 429 | 543 | 419 | 256 |
| **Les Paul Junior 3/4** | — | — | — | — | — | — | 18 | 222 | 181 | 199 | 96 | 71 |
| **Les Paul Special (SG)** | — | — | — | — | — | 373 | 1.345 | 1.452 | 958 | 1.821 | 1.387 | 1.186 |
| **Les Paul Special 3/4 (SG)** | — | — | — | — | — | — | — | — | — | 12 | 39 | 47 |
| **EB 1** | — | — | — | 105 | 125 | 127 | 65 | 79 | 45 | — | — | — |
| **EB O** | — | — | — | — | — | — | — | — | — | 123 | 342 | 535** |
| **Flying V** | — | — | — | — | — | — | — | — | 81 | 17 | — | — |
| **Moderne** | — | — | — | — | — | — | — | — | 19 | 3 | — | — |
| **Melody Maker** | — | — | — | — | — | — | — | — | — | 1.397 | 2.430 | 2.390 |
| **Melody Maker 3/4** | — | — | — | — | — | — | — | — | — | 1.676 | 424 | 225 |
| **Melody Maker D** | — | — | — | — | — | — | — | — | — | — | 1.196 | 1.491 |

* These figures include both the Original Les Paul models and the new SG/Les Paul introduced in 1961.
** This figure includes both the Original EB O and the SG styled model introduced in 1961.

# SHIPPING TOTALS

## "THIN LINE" GUITARS AND BASSES
(including the semi-solid electrics)

| | 1954 | 1955 | 1956 | 1957 | 1958 | 1959 | 1960 | 1961 |
|---|---|---|---|---|---|---|---|---|
| **Byrdland** | — | 1 | 31 | 78 | 38 | 40 | 71 | 77 |
| **Byrdland N** | — | 2 | 25 | 52 | 23 | 34 | 39 | 20 |
| **ES 350 T** | — | 1 | 156 | 150 | 104 | 90 | 71 | 61 |
| **ES 350 TN** | — | 1 | 62 | 74 | 43 | 57 | 15 | 21 |
| **ES 225 T** | — | 467 | 1.463 | 1.192 | 962 | 716 | — | — |
| **ES 225 TN** | — | — | 71 | 138 | 123 | 88 | — | — |
| **ES 225 TD** | — | — | 205 | 582 | 697 | 728 | — | — |
| **ES 225 TDN** | — | — | 23 | 125 | 223 | 171 | — | — |
| **ES 140 T** | — | — | 70 | 443 | 234 | 296 | 116 | 92 |
| **ES 140 TN** | — | — | 8 | 27 | 22 | — | — | — |
| **ES 335 TD** | — | — | — | — | 267 | 521 | 405 | 466 |
| **ES 335 TDN** | — | — | — | — | 50 | 71 | 88 | — |
| **ES 335 TDC** | — | — | — | — | — | — | 21 | 420 |
| **ES 345 TD** | — | — | — | — | — | 446 | 251 | 174 |
| **ES 345 TDN** | — | — | — | — | — | 32 | 18 | — |
| **ES 345 TDC** | — | — | — | — | — | — | 252 | 223 |
| **ES 355 TD** | — | — | — | — | 10 | 177 | 128 | 117 |
| **ES 355 TD SV** | — | — | — | — | — | 123 | 189 | 174 |
| **EB 2** | — | — | — | — | 90 | 203 | 102 | 32 |
| **EB 2 N** | — | — | — | — | 6 | 60 | 17 | — |
| **EB 6** | — | — | — | — | — | — | 34 | 33 |
| **ES 330 T** | — | — | — | — | — | 349 | 772 | 267 |
| **ES 330 TN** | — | — | — | — | — | 82 | 88 | — |
| **ES 330 TC** | — | — | — | — | — | — | 37 | 214 |
| **ES 330 TD** | — | — | — | — | — | 270 | 1.198 | 542 |
| **ES 330 TDN** | — | — | — | — | — | 79 | 215 | — |
| **ES 330 TDC** | — | — | — | — | — | — | 98 | 645 |

# APPENDIX III
# IDENTIFICATION NUMBERS

A Gibson guitar usually carries an identification number, which may actually be either a real **serial number,** meant for the registration of the instrument (mainly for guarantee purposes), or a **factory number** intended for an "internal" use at the plant. At this stage, it is necessary to point out that a Gibson guitar may well carry one of these two numbers, both of them at the same time, or even, neither of the two!

Throughout the years, Gibson instruments have been registered in different ways according to the model and the period. Consequently it is sometimes difficult to deduce from any number the principal indication that most people are today trying to decipher, namely the age of an instrument!

However it would be exaggerated to state that such a number — serial or factory number — has no significance at all, since the type of numeration and its location can already provide "some" information as to the period of manufacture. For instance, no Gibson electric shipped prior to 1961 has a serial number imprinted in the wood on the back of the headstock.

Besides such "limited" information, it is possible, in most cases, to logically interpret the various numbers used by Gibson. This is especially true of all the systems into effect up to 1961, on the models featured in this first volume, but much less so for the numbers used between 1961 and 1977.

As a matter of fact, it must be noted that every instrument is generally registered in the company's records — at least since 1948 — and consequently Gibson is able to trace a guitar in its books on the basis of its type and number (... well in most cases!). Ken Killman has a nice collection of ledgers in his office where thousands of Gibson's can be tracked down! (His phone number is not supplied in the appendix!).

Now the relative difficulty concerning the Gibson numbers for the period we are interested in, comes from their multiplicity and their apparent lack of unity, compared, say to Martin, where a single type of number, increasing in chronological order, is used.

Although we are unable to supply perfect answers to all the questions regarding identification numbers, we will successively examine the five major systems used by Gibson on its electrics between 1935 and 1961.

However it must be remembered that a great number of Gibson instruments — particularly in the 1940's carry no visible numbers. In this case, the evaluation of the age can only be achieved thanks to the specifications and the features of the model.

FIRST IDENTIFICATION SYSTEM

## FACTORY NUMBERS FROM 1935 UP TO 1951

The first "real" Gibson electric guitar to be marketed was the ES 150 in 1936. This guitar was an electrified L 50 considered at that time to be a somewhat bottom of the line with no serial number but only a factory number stamped in ink and pencil on the back of the guitar under the lower "F" hole. The first electric models, the ES 150 and ES 100, were thus similarly labelled with just a factory number, basically reading as follows.

XXX - Y
XXX - YY
XXXX - Y
XXXX - YY
XXXXX - Y
XXXXX - YY

The first 3, 4, or 5 digits (X) indicate the number of the batch to which the instrument belongs. The 1 or 2 following digits (Y) correspond to the rank of the instrument in this batch. Gibson guitars were then most often produced in batches of 35 to 40 units.

Thus, a factory number reading "2620-13" would mean that the instrument was the "13th" in the batch number 2620 corresponding to such and such model... which is perhaps not very explicit, as it is hardly possible to fully identify a batch number after 1923 at least... as far as we know. In fact, from this date onwards, different systems were used according to the various instruments (guitars, mandolins, banjos...) and models. Fortunately, for the period we are dealing with, it seems that Gibson started to insert letters in its factory numbers from about 1935. Reading a list of numbers supplied by the factory allows one to observe a progression in the code letters. The following numbers are listed with the appropriate models opposite.

| | | |
|---|---|---|
| 1935 | 1351-24 | L 50 |
| | 1387-6 | L 50 |
| | 181-A-18 | L 50 |
| | 288-A-13 | L 50 |
| 1936 | 392-A-36 | ES 150 |
| | 96-1-12 | L 37 |
| | 661-B-26 | L 50 |
| | 1098-B-6 | ES 150 |
| 1937 | 123-C-22 | L 37 |
| | 1262-C-42 | L 50 |
| | 1362-C-34 | L 50 |
| | 400-C-19 | L 37 |
| 1938 | DGE-2333 | ES 150 |
| | DG-4590 | L 50 |
| | DG-5272 | L 37 |
| | DGE-5716 | EH 100 |
| | DK-2837 | KG 21 |
| 1939 | EG-4881 | L 30 |
| | EG-6690 | ES 150 |
| | EGE-6860 | EH 150 |
| | EG-7040 | L 50 |
| | EK-3074 | KG 32 |
| 1940 | FG-2770 | L 50 |
| | F-9243 | EH 100 |
| 1941 | 2780-G-19 | ES 100 |
| | 2376-G-38 | ES 125 |

Judging from this list, one can assume the following progression to be accurate, however, this has been neither confirmed nor refuted by Gibson.

| | | |
|---|---|---|
| A = 1935 | D = 1938 | G = 1941 |
| B = 1936 | E = 1939 | |
| C = 1937 | F = 1940 | |

The factory number principle remained the same and the inserted letter only served to determine the year when the manufacturing process started. A similar system will be used again in 1952 (see 4th identification system).

From 1938, the order of the digits of these factory numbers was modified, with the code letter as a prefix and one or two complementary letters. Judging from the numbers we have seen, the second letter is either a "G" or a "K" The letter "G" corresponds to a Gibson model, while "K" indicates a Kalamazoo instrument. When a 3rd letter is present it is always an "E" and it applies to "electric" instruments. For instance DGE 2333 on an ES 150 would mean that the instrument was made in 1938 (D), of Gibson make (G), and electric (E).

Of course, it is difficult to systematically resort to this type of analysis when dealing with factory numbers, mainly because of a lack of information in this matter. However, we consider this system to be reliable for the 1935 to 1941 period.

From 1942, identification possibilities are somewhat more limited, as the practice of a visible factory number disappeared only to be resumed in 1949. As already mentioned, a large number of models made in the forties carry no visible number.

From about 1949, a system identical to the one used before 1935 was reinstored with a number of the XXXX-Y or XXXX-YY type printed on the back of the guitar, under the lower "F" hole.

To illustrate this we are quoting hereunder a few numbers taken from a list supplied by Gibson.

| | | |
|---|---|---|
| 1949 | 2001 - 20 | ES 125 |
| | 2133 - 8 | ES 125 |
| 1950 | 3634 - 5 | L 48 |
| | 4079 - 2 | ES 140 |
| 1951 | 8322 - 36 | L 50 |
| | 9106 - 2 | ES 125 |

Unfortunately, we don't know of any information today which would allow us to date these numbers accurately, and in fact the factory number is of little use in this respect.

The factory numbers for the 1935 to 1941 period apply to both acoustic and electric instruments, but on the electric models they may be found on the following guitars (without any serial number), up to around 1951 : ES 100, ES 125, ES 150, ES 140, CF 100 E.

Starting in 1952, a new system with a different code letter was adopted. This system is currently termed as "Reverse Alphabetical Order" and we will examine it more closely at a later stage (see the 4th identification system).

### SECOND IDENTIFICATION SYSTEM

# SERIAL NUMBERS FROM 1935 TO 1947

The first serial number system used by the Gibson Mandolin Guitar Mfg. Co. Ltd. appeared in 1903. It was characterized by a 4 or 5 digit figure printed, along with the type of instrument, on a white, paper label which served as the guarantee. This label was visible through the round sound-hole on the early models. Then, with the appearance of "F" hole guitars the label became oval and glued on the back of the instrument under the upper "F" hole.

However, a guitar carrying a serial number also had a factory number. On models with a round sound-hole the factory number was placed on the dovetail block, while on guitars with "F" holes, it was ink-stamped under the lower "F" hole.

The first electric guitars to be commercialized (ES 150, ES 100) did not carry a "real" serial number and consequently they cannot be found in the series starting in 1903. The ES 250 — i.e. the third electric model made during the pre-War period — was the first electric to be registered in this series. It appeared for the first time in the 1940 "AA" catalog, but it is possible though that a few of them were already released by the end of 1939. Therefore we will start the series with 1939 numbers for the sake of information.

At the beginning of 1947 five digit numbers were stopped when the series reached the crucial "99999" figure. According to the Gibson records this number was attributed to an "L 7" registered on April 28th 1947. The "A" series (see 3rd identification system) came into effect as from this date, to replace the former system.

The only electric models to use the 5 digit system between 1935 and 1947 were the ES 250 and ES 300. It is possible however that the very first ES 350 carried a similar number, but we have never come across any. The numbers in this series seem reasonably consecutive, but judging from the information we have gathered, some of them did occasionely overlap or repeat, and thus a few discrepancies may arise.

The following list was compiled from Gibson documents and it does help the identification of a model of this period, even though it may offer recognizable features likely to determine the year of production.

| | | |
|---|---|---|
| 1939 | 95884 | L 7 |
| | 95923 | Super 400 |
| 1940 | 96090 | L 7 |
| | 96091 | ES 250 |
| | 96141 | Super 400 |
| | 96460 | L 7 |
| 1941 | 96885 | ES 300 |
| | 96932 | ES 300 |
| | 96987 | ES 300 |
| | 97321 | ES 300 |
| 1942 | 97384 | L 5 |
| | 97479 | Super 400 |
| | 97535 | L 4 |
| | 97618 | ES 300 |

| | | |
|---|---|---|
| 1943 | 97709 | L 7 |
| | 97718 | L 7 |
| 1944 | 97951 | L 7 |
| | 98150 | L 7 |
| 1945 | 98343 | L 7 |
| | 98398 | L 7 |
| | 98567 | L 5 |
| | 98603 | ES 300 |
| 1946 | 98660 | L 4 |
| | 98970 | L 5 |
| | 99214 | L 7 |
| | 99314 | L 5 |
| 1947 | 99329 | L 7 |
| | 99554 | L 7 |
| | 99760 | L 7 |
| | 99999 | L 7 (on April 28th 1947) |

A few "top-models" made during the pre-War period were incidentally supplied with numbers unknown to this series. Although they were indicated on a white oval label, glued under the upper "F" hole, these numbers looked somewhat like factory numbers. However they were not, as the instruments on which such numbers can be found also had a distinct factory number under the lower "F" hole. The following examples were compiled on acoustic guitars made around 1939 :

| | |
|---|---|
| EA 5173 | L 5 N |
| EA 5196 | L 4 |
| EA 5381 | Super 400 |
| EA 5466 | L 7 |

It does not seem, though, that this numbering scheme was ever used on an electric guitar, but we chose to mention them as a matter of interest in this study.

THIRD IDENTIFICATION SYSTEM

# SERIAL NUMBERS FROM 1947 TO 1961

## FOR ACOUSTIC AND SEMI-SOLID GUITARS

After the 5 digit series ran out in 1947 Gibson started using a new series characterized by the prefix "A". The serial number and the type of the instrument were still printed on a white oval label, which was stuck on the bottom of the guitar and visible as before through the upper "F" hole.

Contrary to what is usually believed this series is quite accurate as regards the date of issue of a guitar since the numbers were chronologically recorded in the Gibson ledgers at Kalamazoo. We were able to consult the two books in which the "A" numbers are registered and the list which follows shows the first numbers used in January and July of each year with the model involved. The dates listed opposite correspond to the registration day after the instrument was manufactured. This list applies particularly to the following electric models : ES 300, ES 350, L-7 E, L-7 CE, L-7 ED, L-7 CED, ES-5, ES-175, L-5 CES, SUPER 400 CES, ES-295, ES-175 D, ES-5 Switchmaster, Byrdland, ES-350 T, ES-335, EB-2, ES-355, ES-345, EB-6, L-4 CE.

The first number — A 100 — was registered on April 28th 1947 and the series continued until early 1961 when the last number used was A 36147 for an L 5 CES. We did notice however that the series was printed in the Gibson books up to A 36455 but it looks as though numbers A 36148 to A 36455 were never used on a guitar... at least it was not recorded in the books ! The type of instrument and the registration date are shown for each number :

| | | |
|---|---|---|
| A 100 | L 7 | April 28th 1947 |
| A 411 | L 7 | July 2nd 1947 |
| A 1305 | L 12 P | January 8th 1948 |
| A 1849 | L 5 | July 2nd 1948 |
| A 2666 | L 7 | January 5th 1949 |
| A 3353 | ES 350 | July 1st 1949 |
| A 4414 | ES 175 | January 3rd 1950 |
| A 5456 | L 7 | July 3rd 1950 |
| A 6598 | ES 175 N | January 4th 1951 |
| A 8030 | ES 350 | July 2nd 1951 |
| A 9420 | Super 400 CES | January 2nd 1952 |
| A 11057 | ES 175 | July 1st 1952 |
| A 12463 | J 185 | January 8th 1953 |
| A 14332 | ES 175 | July 1st 1953 |
| A 16102 | L 5 C | January 5th 1954 |
| A 17435 | J 200 | July 1st 1954 |
| A 18668 | ES 295 | January 6th 1955 |
| A 20991 | ES 175 N | July Ist 1955 |

| | |
|---|---|
| A 21910 L 7 C | January 6th 1956 |
| A 23387 J 200 | July 3rd 1956 |
| A 24756 L 7 C | January 3rd 1957 |
| A 25899 ES 5 Switch. | July 3rd 1957 |
| A 26820 ES 5 Switch. | January 6th 1958 |
| A 27816 Super 400 CES | July 1st 1958 |
| A 28881 J 200 | January 9th 1959 |
| A 30569 EB 2 | July 13th 1959 |
| A 32285 ES 335 T | January 4th 1960 |
| A 34068 J 200 | July 1st 1960 |
| A 35646 Hummingbird | January 3rd 1961 |
| A 36147 L 5 CES | February 21st 1961 |

Up to 1954 the serial number was indicated on a white oval label then afterwards on an orange oval label. Furthermore, as already mentioned the models with an "A" serial number did also carry a factory number that can be seen through the lower "F" hole.

Starting in February of 1961, Gibson used a new identification system with 3, then 4, 5 and finally 6 digits, as a serial number. This number was then systematically imprinted in the wood, on the back of the headstock. However during the sixties this new serial number was also printed on the orange oval label stuck inside the guitar body under the upper "F" hole, thus the serial number could be seen in two different places.

FOURTH IDENTIFICATION SYSTEM

# FACTORY NUMBERS FROM 1952 TO 1961

A new type of factory number was introduced as from 1952, on all the acoustic and semi-solid guitars. This system is commonly called "reverse alphabetical order" because the numbers carry a prefix letter which from 1952 onwards is in "reverse" alphabetical order, that is, beginning with a "Z". These numbers are nonetheless similar to the previous factory numbers with the exception of the prefix, and show a 3 or 4 digit root corresponding to the number of the batch, and a suffix of 1 or 2 digits indicating the rank of the model in the batch.

The key-letters for each year are the following :

| | | |
|---|---|---|
| Z : 1952 | V : 1956 | R : 1960 |
| Y : 1953 | U : 1957 | Q : 1961 |
| X : 1954 | T : 1958 | |
| W : 1955 | S : 1959 | |

The numbers were ink-stamped on the back of the guitar under the lower "F" hole or the round sound-hole for models like the J 160 E. This system was used in conjunction with "A" serial numbers and it is therefore particularly helpful for identifying electric models which carry no other number, such as :

ES-140, ES-140 T, CF-100 E, ES-125, ES-150, ES-135, J-160 E, ES-225 T, ES-225 TD, ES-125 T, ES-125 TD, ES-330 T, ES-330 TD, ES-125 TC, ES-125 TCD.

For all these models the factory number based on the reverse alphabetical system can be used to determine the year of manufacture although overlapping from one year to the other may occur. In other words a number which begins with a "Z" may belong to a model which was actually started in 1952 (hence the letter "Z") but completed only in 1953 (letter "Y").

In order to illustrate this system here are some factory numbers taken from a list supplied by Gibson.

| | | |
|---|---|---|
| 1952 | Z-2170-28 | ES 125 |
| 1953 | Y-5202-10 | CF 100 E |
| 1954 | X-9120-27 | ES 140 |
| 1955 | W-2833-33 | J 160 E |
| 1956 | V-8032-11 | ES 225 TD |
| 1957 | U- 691-30 | ES 140 T |
| 1958 | T-3664-14 | ES 125 T |
| 1959 | S-1028-17 | ES 330 T |
| 1960 | R-3923-12 | ES 125 T |

Moreover we have selected a few instruments which carry two different numbers, to clearly show the distinction between serial and factory numbers. After the type of model, we have indicated the serial number (upper "F" hole), and the factory number (lower "F" hole) :

| | |
|---|---|
| ES 175 | A 11967 and Z 2145-7 |
| ES 295 | A 17387 and Y 6685-21 |
| ES 295 | A 20238 and X 362-10 |

| | | | | |
|---|---|---|---|---|
| Super 400 CESN | A 22045 | and | W | 1508-9 |
| Super 400 C | A 24669 | and | V | 4383-10 |
| L 5 CES | A 26147 | and | U | 8952-1 |
| ES 355 TD/SV | A 30677 | and | S | 7625-34 |
| ES 350 T | A 36000 | and | R | 6078-2 |

It is interesting to note that factory numbers were stamped inside the box in the early stages of the manufacturing process while "A" serial numbers were applied and registered once the instruments were finished and ready to be shipped. The ES-350 T listed above is a good example to further illustrate this point since its factory number — beginning with an "R" — suggests it was made in 1960 while its serial number (A 36000) was actually registered in the Gibson ledgers on February 9th, 1961 ! Both numbers are usually a few months apart.

According to Gibson, the "reverse alphabetical order" was officially stopped in 1963 with the letter "O", but as early as 1961 such factory numbers are no longer visible on most electric guitars of the period. However this is not exceedingly disturbing since the models which up to that time did not have a real serial number, were lined up with the rest of the Gibson range and supplied with a 3 to 6 digit serial number imprinted in the wood on the peg-head.

Lastly, a few transitional models registered in February 1961, are known to exhibit three (yes 3 !) different numbers, namely one factory number and two distinct serial numbers. The first serial number belongs to the "A" series and is located under the upper "F" hole while a second serial number is actually imprinted on the back of the headstock, and bears no relationship whatsoever to the "A" number. For instance, we came across an ES 335 TD with "A 36127" on the orange oval label and "2413" on the peg-head, whereas the factory number under the lower "F" hole was reading "R 8025-35".

In all likelihood, the "A" series was suddenly interrupted by the end of February 1961 with number A-36147 — although it was already printed in advance in the Gibson books up to number A-36455 — so that the two visible serial numbers (i.e. on the paper label and behind the headstock) correctly matched !

FIFTH IDENTIFICATION SYSTEM

# SERIAL NUMBERS FROM 1953 TO 1961

## FOR SOLID-BODY GUITARS

The different systems that we have examined until now do not relate to solid body guitars which were first marketed in 1952. In fact, it is only in 1953 that Gibson decided to supply its solid-body electrics with a serial number. Because of its structure it was hardly feasible to stick a label with a serial number on such an instrument. Gibson therefore decided to ink stamp a number under the varnish, behind the headstock of each solid-body. This system proved to be original and easy to understand, as the first figure in the serial number corresponds to the last figure of the year of manufacture. The remaining four or five digits approximately determined the appearance of the model in the course of the year.

We can therefore assume that a solid-body guitar carrying an 8-3867 number was actually manufactured in 1958.

This system was applied to all the solid-body guitars and basses as well as electric Hawaiian guitars. The number was stamped with black or yellow ink, depending on the finish of the instrument. With a clear finish the number was in black, whereas with a dark finish it was in yellow. Initially, the number following the reference figure for the year had 4 digits, but by the end of the year when Gibson had more or less used up all the digit possibilities a 5th digit was inserted between the two parts of the number. Thus a model with a number 512699 was certainly manufactured at the end of 1955.

The numbering scheme used on solid-body guitars starting in 1953 is therefore very simple and consistent, and only models made in 1952 and at the beginning of 1953 do not carry a number of this kind... but they are nonetheless easy to identify because of their particulars e.g. Les Paul Gold Top with a trapeze bridge/tailpiece combination.

To better illustrate this system, we have selected a few examples of serial numbers between 1953 and 1961 with listed opposite the models they were taken from :

| | | |
|---|---|---|
| 1953 | 3-0915 | Les Paul Model (with trapeze bridge/tailpiece combination) |
| | 3-2068 | Les Paul Model (with a stop tailpiece) |
| | 3-2675 | Electric Bass |
| 1954 | 4-0378 | Les Paul Model |
| | 4-1576 | Les Paul Model |
| | 4-4119 | Les Paul Junior |
| 1955 | 5-6350 | Electric Bass |
| | 5-11587 | Les Paul Custom |
| | 5-12975 | Les Paul Special |
| 1956 | 6-3562 | Les Paul Custom |
| | 6-12672 | Les Paul Model |
| | 6-14805 | Les Paul Special |
| 1957 | 7-0743 | Les Paul Model (with white single coil pick-ups) |
| | 7-3956 | Les Paul Model (with Humbucking pick-ups) |
| | 7-8440 | Les Paul Junior |
| 1958 | 8-2846 | Flying V |
| | 8-4545 | Explorer |
| | 8-6907 | Les Paul Standard (with "Cherry Sunburst" finish) |
| 1959 | 9-0144 | Les Paul-Custom |
| | 9-1945 | Les Paul-Standard |
| | 9-10857 | Les Paul Junior (with a double cutaway) |
| 1960 | 0-0266 | Les Paul Standard |
| | 0-1911 | Les Paul Junior |
| | 0-8498 | EB 0 |
| 1961 | 1-0359 | Les Paul Special (actually a SGR Special) |
| | 1-0925 | Melody Maker |
| | 1-1055 | Les Paul Custom |

Note there was no dash between the first digit and the rest of the number, when it was actually ink-stamped on the guitar.

These "date-numbers" were used on solid bodies until the beginning of 1961, when serial numbers impressed into the wood started to appear on the whole Gibson range. The very first solid body electrics with such a number stamped **into the wood** (as opposed to rubber stamped) were registered as early as February 1961. However, we were able to find in the Gibson ledgers several models with an inked-on number, registered at a later date! In fact, the original Les Paul models were available in the early part of 1961 with both numbers. This may seem "ordinary" if the ink-stamped numbers look like "1-0808" (Les Paul Junior) or "1-1067" (Les Paul Custom), however, a "Les Paul Special" with a "922407" number (= 1959) officially registered (shipped?) on August 1961 is rather strange!!!

On the solid body instruments the serial number was ink-stamped on the back of the headstock from 1953 up to early 1961.

In any case both systems overlapped in 1961 until the inked-on numbers fell into disuse, although a few instruments with the old style numbers were held in stock and shipped at a later date (e.g. Flying V and Explorer).

In 1961 the various identification systems we have so far examined were replaced by a unique system common to all Gibson models. From 1961 onwards all Gibson instruments began to carry a serial number with 3, then 4, 5 and finally 6 digits. This number was then systematically imprinted in the wood on the back of the headstock of each instrument. As a matter of fact, any guitar with such a number could not have been shipped prior to 1961.

# INDEX OF PHOTOGRAPHS


| | |
|---|---|
| *Front cover photographs by* | *Dany Giorgetti* |
| *Back cover photographs by* | *Dany Giorgetti*<br>*Claude Gassian*<br>*André Duchossoir* |
| *Color photographs supplied by* | *Dany Giorgetti, 25, 29, 31, 32, 65, 66, 72 (top left and right), 121, 123, 126, 127, 128, 146, 150*<br>*André Duchossoir, 26, 27, 28, 30, 72 (center), 122, 124, 125, 128 (top left)*<br>*Claude Gassian, 67, 68, 70 (top left), 147, 148, 149, 151*<br>*Tony Dukes, 69*<br>*Frank Lucido, 70*<br>*Robb Lawrence, 71*<br>*Jean-Pierre Leloir, 145*<br>*Jean-Louis Rancurel, 152* |

*Black and white photographs and other illustrations supplied by*

*André Duchossoir, 5, 7, 17, 21, 38, 42, 43, 45, 48, 51, 59, 74, 75, 80, 85, 86, 90, 96, 101, 102, 106, 107, 110, 113, 116, 130, 133, 138, 143, 154, 157, 159, 167*

*Dany Giorgetti, 3, 5, 16, 17, 40, 47, 59, 62, 79, 82, 99, 106, 107, 110, 116, 154, 157, 187*

*George Gruhn, 51, 77, 85, 95, 96, 99, 116, 140, 159*

*Claude Gassian, 45, 74, 75, 77, 95, 140, 155*

*Tony Dukes, 75, 79, 80, 95*

*Robb Lawrence, 47, 115, 140, 143*

*Jean-Louis Rancurel, 80, 109, 116*

*Concord Jazz Records, 40, 45, 130*

*Herschel Blankenship, 131, 155*

*Julius Bellson, 3, 13*

*Jean-Pierre Leloir, 45, 51*

*Frank Lucido, 92*

*Norman Mongan, 118*

*Doug Chandler, 131*

*Atlantic Records, 82*

*Warner Records, 139*

*Reproduction from GIBSON literature and documents supplied by GIBSON Inc.*
*3, 5, 7, 16, 19, 21, 23, 38, 40, 42, 48, 51, 57, 74, 77, 80, 85, 92, 101, 106, 109, 113, 118, 119, 130, 131, 133, 142, 143, 154, 155*

*Special Acknowledgement for the second printing"*
*Many thanks to George Gruhn and Tom Wheeler for their help in correcting a lot of typos and mistakes contained in the first printing.*

# ALPHABETIC INDEX

First printing: November 1981